Beyond Interpr

Beyond Interpretation:

The Meaning of Hermeneutics for Philosophy

GIANNI VATTIMO

Translated by David Webb

Polity Press

English translation copyright © Polity Press 1997
First published as *Oltre l'interpretazione*
copyright © 1994 Gius. Laterza and Figli S.p.A., Roma-Bari.
This book comes of the cooperation between Laterza Publishing House
and Sigma-Tau Foundation in the 'Lezioni Italiane' series.
English language edition arranged through the mediation of
Eulama Literary Agency.
Appendix 1 copyright © Gius. Laterza & Figli 1989
Appendix 2 copyright © Gius. Laterza & Figli 1992

This translation first published in 1997 by Polity Press
in association with Blackwell Publishers Ltd.

Editorial office:
Polity Press
65 Bridge Street
Cambridge CB2 1UR, UK

Marketing and production:
Blackwell Publishers Ltd
108 Cowley Road
Oxford OX4 1JF, UK

ISBN 0-7456-1567-8
ISBN 0-7456-1753-0 (pbk)

A CIP catalogue record for this book is available from the British Library.

Typeset in 11 on 13 pt Sabon
by CentraCet Ltd, Cambridge
Printed in Great Britain by
T.J. Press Ltd, Padstow, Cornwall

This book is printed on acid-free paper

Oft denk' ich, sie sind nur ausgegangen!
Bald werden sie wieder nach Hause gelangen!
Der Tag ist schön! O sei nicht bang!
Sie machen nur einen weiten Gang.

F. Rückert, *Kindertotenlieder*

In memory of Gianpiero Cavaglià

Contents

Preface

This book is prompted by a certain unease. In contemporary philosophy, hermeneutics has begun to acquire an 'ecumenical' form so vague and generic that, in my view, it is losing much of its meaning. In particular, it is becoming increasingly difficult to say what significance hermeneutics has for the problems of which philosophy has traditionally spoken: problems such as those of science, ethics, religion and art. Trying to shed light on these borderline problems, as they might be called, leads us to rethink the 'originary' meaning of hermeneutics that, as I have attempted to make clear in chapter 1, is to be found in its 'nihilistic vocation'. Elsewhere in recent years I have spoken in this respect of 'weak thought'. The reflections presented here should serve – in lieu of a larger work (announced previously as *The Game of Interpretation*, and then, which at present I consider its definitive title, as *Ontology of Actuality*) – also to dispel various equivocalities that have accumulated around the meaning of that theoretical proposal, above all due to the notion of weakness having been taken in too narrow and literal a sense. At bottom, the same equivocalities are attached to nihilism, though on a plane vaster in proportion to weight of the term's historical associations. The itinerary followed in these five chapters, whose schematic and programmatic tone I readily acknowledge, leads in a direction that might be seen as scandalous, in that it 'twists' weakness and nihilism into a sense totally different to the usual: and above all, because it ends somehow in the arms of theology – albeit in ways that do not bring it into contact with any 'orthodoxy'.

These pages therefore contain a number of significant new departures (for me) regarding hermeneutics, weak thought and nihilism that will, I hope, at least contribute to calling attention back to the problem, as the subtitle says, of the meaning of hermeneutics for philosophy. I am pleased to have been able to present these reflections in the series of 'Lezioni Italiane' organized by the Sigma-Tau Foundation and the Laterza Publishing House (to whom I am very grateful), not only in view of the solemnity of the occasion, but also because the cycle of lessons were hosted at the University of Bologna by Umberto Eco, an old friend who has also been a kind of old comrade or vice-maestro in the school of Luigi Pareyson in which we both were trained and of which, albeit in different ways, our work bears deep signs of influence. In the week in which these papers were presented, Eco came in my eyes to assume a 'magisterial' role both in himself and in his capacity as representative of the school to which it felt as though I were presenting myself for a comprehensive examination of my position. All this has little, it is true, to do with the 'thing itself'; I recall it only because it might explain, and justify, the schematic and programmatic tone that may seem to be a limitation of the book. To Eco and to all those who participated in the discussions in Bologna (raising several of the points that came together in the notes) I extend my warmest thanks and acknowledgement. By way of a response to a number of problems arising from the discussions, as well as to broaden my argumentation on various points, there is an appendix containing two essays previously published in the annual journal that I edit for the same publishing house (in *Filosofia '88* and *Filosofia '91* respectively). Finally, I would like to say thank you to my friends and collaborators Luca Bagetto, Luca D'Isanto and Giuseppe Iannantuono for their intelligent help in the final preparation of this book.

G.V.

1

The Nihilistic Vocation of Hermeneutics

The hypothesis of the mid-eighties that hermeneutics had become a sort of *koiné* or common idiom of Western culture, and not only of philosophy, seems yet to have been refuted.[1] This may of course be due, at least in part, to its being a weak hypothesis that does not affirm a great many precise shared philosophical beliefs, but rather describes an overall climate, a general sensibility, or simply a kind of presupposition that everyone feels more or less obliged to take into account. In this very generic sense, which bears no more precise definition, not only are Heidegger, Gadamer, Ricoeur and Pareyson hermeneutic thinkers, but so are Habermas and Apel, Rorty and Charles Taylor, Jacques Derrida and Emmanuel Levinas. What links these writers is not a common thesis but rather what Wittgenstein (another hermeneutic thinker in the broad sense intended here) called a family resemblance; or, more modestly still, a sense of family, a common atmosphere.

Without developing this observation any further here (which would in any case be both impossible and unnecessary), I take it as a point of departure because the pervasiveness of hermeneutics seems to have come about at the expense of a dilution of its original philosophical meaning. It is hard to see how hermeneutics defined so broadly as to include writers as different among themselves as those mentioned above could have 'consequences': it ends up as something innocuous, worthless even. I also set aside the question, that could be debated at length, of whether it is legitimate in philosophy to lead a theory as vague and pervasive as hermeneutics has become in our hypothesis back to its authentic, original and essential meaning. Theories do not have patents or brand names, still less theories such as the one we are speaking of here which was born precisely, and this is not to say a great deal, in order to affirm the rights of interpretation. And yet it is quite legitimate for those referring to a school, theory or current of thinking to try to preserve aspects of its meaning that they believe to be important, characteristic or decisive with respect to problems that are widely debated and dear to them. (In any case, the rights of translation comprise the freedom to reconstruct a given *de facto* historical form – a work, or a philosophy – referring back as rigorously as possible to its internal legality, to what Pareyson calls the 'forming form';[2] the freedom of interpretation is anything but arbitrary and brings with it risk and responsibility.) There is no attempt here to rediscover authenticity, to affirm a right exclusive to the name or the brand, or to correspond as faithfully as possible to the original intention of the author. It is simply a matter of not hastening to lay aside a patrimony of ideas that – on the basis of a particular determination of what we have found there – looks as though it could be more fruitful than it is at present.

If, as good hermeneuticians, we go on to admit that there are no facts, but only interpretations, then what we are proposing is precisely an interpretation of the philosophical meaning of hermeneutics – not, however, one opposed to another specific interpretation that might underlie the general hermeneutic *koiné*. Rather, our interpretation infers from the extent of the current popularity of hermeneutics in its various forms that it can appear so acceptable, urbane and harmless only because it lacks philosophical precision.

What then do we call hermeneutics and how do we identify its (in my view constitutive) nihilistic vocation? For ease of exposition, yet (as we shall see) also for more substantial theoretical reasons, we shall define hermeneutics as that philosophy developed along the Heidegger–Gadamer axis. The series of problems and solutions elaborated by these authors comprise all aspects of twentieth-century hermeneutics and the different paths taken by it. Heidegger and Gadamer, in other words, are not the only great figures of twentieth-century hermeneutics (alongside them one would have at least to place Pareyson and Ricoeur), and nor do they constitute a unitary theoretical block in which the essential principles of this philosophy may be found. To speak of axes and series, with all the vagueness this brings (corresponding, albeit in more rigorous terms, to the vague sense assumed by hermeneutics in becoming *koiné*), means recognizing that these authors represent the poles of a tension, the extreme limits of a picture in which, nearer to one or the other, all the authors generally included in this current are to be found. So if one cannot say that hermeneutics is Heidegger and Gadamer, taking these authors as its defining limits is nonetheless a good way to picture it. Seen thus, hermeneutics reveals its constitutive characteristics: those of ontology and *Sprachlichkeit*, linguisticality. In spite of all the emphasis that Heidegger places on language, especially in the later phase of his thought, he regards interpretation primarily from the point of view of the meaning of Being: in spite of all the emphasis that Gadamer places on ontology, interpretation is thought primarily from the point of view of language. Although something of a simplification, the same conclusion is reached whether one takes seriously Habermas's felicitous remark that Gadamer 'urbanized the Heideggerian province', or whether, making sense of this expression, one notes that certain themes which are central to Heidegger, such as distancing oneself from metaphysics as the forgetting of Being, seem in Gadamer to have disappeared completely. Looking for a similar thesis in Gadamer, one finds only the critique of scientism and modern methodologism from which, on the basis of the truth of the experience of art, *Truth and Method* defends a notion of truth broader than (and perhaps antithetical to) that delimited by scientific method.[3] As will become clear later, the intention here is not to return to Heidegger in a reversal of the Gadamerian urbanization. On the contrary, there is a decisive need to urbanize Heidegger's thought in many senses (to the point of its encounter with Rorty's neo-pragmatism). But such urbanization will be truly successful only if one does not forget the specifically Heideggerian ontological aspect of the discourse.

If, keeping these general introductory indications in mind, we are to make progress towards the definition before us – of hermeneutics as a philosophical orientation that is today very widespread and for this very reason somewhat ill-defined, and that we propose to view primarily with regard to the Heidegger–Gadamer arc – we should probably begin with the sense to which the term hermeneutics or the theory of interpretation itself alludes. Whereas, up to a certain point in the history of European culture, the word hermeneutics was always accompanied by an adjective – biblical, juridical, literary or even simply general – in contemporary thought it has begun to appear in its own right. This is not only because the idea has prevailed that the theory of interpretation cannot be otherwise than general, without specialist fields and territories (or at bottom simply non-specialized), but also because it is hermeneutics itself that lost touch with a limited and specific field of phenomena – as though alongside interpretative activity there were another sector of a different kind of activity, such as scientific knowledge. This can be seen clearly in Gadamer's *Truth and Method*, which explicitly takes as its point of departure the problem of the truth of those forms of knowledge, like the human sciences, that are not reducible to positive-scientific method, and ends by constructing a general theory of interpretation in which it coincides with every possible human experience of the world.

It is probably this transition that we should bear in mind in order to understand what we are talking about when we speak of hermeneutics. The generalization of the notion of interpretation to the point where it coincides with the very experience of the world is in fact the result of a transformation in the way we conceive of truth that characterizes hermeneutics as *koiné* and which lays the basis for those general philosophical 'consequences' that we are seeking to illustrate here.

Not only, to stay with the title of *Truth and Method*, is there truth outside the confines of scientific method, but there is no experience of truth that is not interpretative. While this thesis is shared by all those who espouse hermeneutics, and is even widely accepted by the greater part of twentieth-century thought (it is the very meaning of the *koiné*), its implications for the conception of Being are less generally recognized. To reformulate my programme in this book, this is the birthplace of that vagueness of hermeneutics which borders on and often breaches the bounds of vacuity and obviousness, in such a way as to seem almost a deliberate attempt to exorcize the significance of hermeneutics for philosophy.[4]

That each experience of truth is an experience of interpretation is almost a truism in today's culture. As a thesis, it represents the outcome not only of early twentieth-century existentialism, but also of earlier neo-Kantianism, phenomenology and even of neo-positivist and analytic thought. If propositions may be verified or falsified by the conformity or otherwise of statements to states of things, this is only possible, in Heideggerian terms, because both statement and thing are in a relation originally made possible by an 'opening' that is not itself the object of a description that can be verified or falsified other than by placing it within an opening that is 'superior', more original etc. I will not recast this thesis in the language of phenomenology, analytic philosophy, Wittgenstein (one would obviously have to refer here to the Wittgensteinian thesis that the reasonableness of language is founded on rules that in turn refer to a form of life, rather than to a correspondence of any kind) or Kuhnian epistemology.[5] If there is a significant disparity between those who more or less explicitly share an understanding of the experience of truth as interpretative in character, it is exemplified in the difference between existentialism and neo-Kantianism. One can in fact regard – still with Heidegger – every experience of truth as an interpretative articulation of a pre-understanding in which we all find ourselves by virtue of the very fact of existing as Being-in-the-world, and yet maintain that the pre-understanding be structural and constitutive of our humanity as such, of a reason the same for all (like the forms of the Kantian transcendental a priori). A careful reading of the first volume of Cassirer's *The Philosophy of Symbolic Forms* (which came out in 1923 and is dedicated to language) would reveal clear parallels between the neo-Kantian approach and that of hermeneutics, marking the differences and, in my view, the wholly unsustainable character of the transcendentalist position.[6]

This is, I am sure, evidence enough of how far the idea of a link or 'identity' between truth and interpretation has spread throughout twentieth-century thought. It is perhaps a sign that this thought shares in a Kantian formation; and this reference to the Kantian heritage itself reveals, in Cassirer for example, that the coherence of hermeneutics with its own source will be at risk if the recognition of truth as interpretation understands this to mean that it is provisional and destined to dissolve in a final restoration of conformity – for example in a true, conforming and transparent description of the structure of symbolizing activity. Cassirer's reproof to Hegel in *The Philosophy of Symbolic Forms*[7] – that he allowed himself to be led by logical symbolization to place absolute spirit at the summit of his philosophy – holds in a certain sense for Cassirer himself. For by restating an evolutionary conception of symbolic forms that opens teleologically onto the 'perfect' symbolism of scientific conceptuality, he reveals what remains, even today, the true problem of the hermeneutic *koiné*: that of coming radically to terms with the historicity and finitude of pre-understanding, with Heidegger's *Geworfenheit*.

What reduces hermeneutics to a generic philosophy of culture is the wholly metaphysical claim (often implicit and unrecognized) to be a finally true description of the (permanent) 'interpretative structure' of human existence. The contradictory character of this claim must be taken seriously and a rigorous reflection on the historicity of hermeneutics, in both senses of the genitive, developed on the basis of it. Hermeneutics is not only a theory of the historicity (horizons) of truth: it is itself a radically historical truth. It cannot think of itself metaphysically as a description of one objective structure of existence amongst others, but only as the response to a sending, to what Heidegger calls *Ge-Schick*. The reasons for preferring a hermeneutic conception of truth to a metaphysical one lie in the historical legacy of which we venture an interpretation and to which we give a response. The example which seems to me most illuminating for an argument of this kind is Nietzsche's announcement of the death of God, which is not a way of expressing a metaphysical 'thesis' poetically and in 'images'. Nietzsche is not trying to say that God is dead because we have finally realized that 'objectively he does not exist' or that reality is such that he is excluded from it. Nietzsche cannot make a statement like this, at least not if we are to read him in line with his theory of interpretation; there are no facts, only interpretations, and of course this too is an interpretation . . .[8] The announcement of the death of God is truly an announcement. Or, in our terms, an acknowledgement of a course of events in which we are implicated and that we do not describe objectively, but interpret speculatively as concluding in the recognition that God is no longer necessary. The hermeneutic complexity of all this consists in the fact that God is not necessary, is revealed as a superfluous lie (a lie precisely because superfluous) by virtue of the transformations wrought in our individual and social existence by our very belief in him. Nietzsche's reasoning is well known: humanity needed the God of metaphysics in order to organize a social existence that was ordered, secure and not continually exposed to the threats of nature – conquered by the construction of a social hierarchy – and of internal drives, tamed by a religiously sanctioned morality. But today this work of reassurance is, if only relatively speaking, complete and we live in a formal and ordered social world, in which science and technology are available to rid our stay in the world of the terror that belonged to primitive man. God seems too extreme, barbaric and excessive a hypothesis. And, moreover, the God that has served as this principle of stability and reassurance is also the one that has always forbidden the lie; so it is to obey him that the faithful have forsworn even that lie which he is himself: it is the faithful that have killed God . . .

Who could present this complex, giddy argument as a poetic statement of the (metaphysical) non-existence of God? Even if one sees that in the end the faithful 'kill' God in the recognition that he is a lie, and therefore that he 'is not there', along with him they also negate the value of truth, which is, in Nietzsche's view, simply another name for God. The 'true world' that becomes a fable (as the title of a well-known chapter of the *Twilight of the Idols* has it) in no sense gives way to a more profound and reliable truth; it gives way to a play of interpretations that is presented philosophically, in its turn, as no more than an interpretation.

The reference to Nietzsche's announcement draws us closer to the theme of nihilism. If hermeneutics, as the philosophical theory of the interpretative character of every experience of truth, is lucid about itself as no more than an interpretation, will it not find itself inevitably caught up in the nihilistic logic of Nietzsche's hermeneutics? This 'logic' may be encapsulated in the statement that there can be no recognition of the essentially interpretative character of the experience of the true without the death of God and without the fabling of the world or, which amounts to the same thing, of Being. In short, it seems impossible to prove the truth of hermeneutics other than by presenting it as the response to a history of Being interpreted as the occurrence of nihilism.

In fact if hermeneutics is not accepted as a comfortable meta-theory of the universality of interpretative phenomena, as a sort of view from nowhere of the perennial conflict, or play, of interpretations, the (only, I believe) alternative is to think the philosophy of interpretation as the final stage in a series of events (theories, vast social and cultural transformations, technologies and scientific 'discoveries'), as the conclusion of a history we feel unable to tell (interpret) except in the terms of nihilism that we find for the first time in Nietzsche.

If hermeneutics were only the discovery of the *fact* that there are different perspectives on the 'world', or on Being, the conception of truth as the objective mirroring of how things are (in this case, of the *fact* that there are multiple perspectives) would be confirmed, whereas it is actually rebutted by the philosophy of interpretation. In this framework, to accept hermeneutics as an interpretation and not as a metaphysical description would, strictly speaking, amount to no more than a matter of taste; indeed not even that, for it would be a case not of choosing but simply of registering a state of mind that remained as wholly inexplicable to oneself as to others (precisely because intractable to argument).

The arguments for a hermeneutic theory of truth are well known: the proposal that truth as correspondence is secondary, and that that there must be an opening prior to the verification or falsification of any proposition; the recognition (existentialist, and before that Nietzschean, but in certain respects also positivist: cf. Spencer) of the finitude, and thus historicity and contingency of primary truth; the claim that the subject is not the bearer of the Kantian a priori, but the heir to a finite-historical language that makes possible and conditions the access of the subject to itself and to the world.

These steps, linked by the reflection of modern hermeneutics upon the problematic of the human sciences (for it is precisely at the point where experimental science and the conception of truth connected to method run up against their limits that the interpretative character of every experience of truth comes to light, along with the historicity of the openings within which all that is true may be given) seem, however, to lead only to what one might call hermeneutics as the metatheory of the play of interpretations. The further step for which the thesis proposed here calls is that of asking whether such a metatheory is not bound to undertake a more radical recognition of its own historicity, its own formal character as interpretation, eliminating the final metaphysical equivocality that stands as a threat to it and which is apt to make of it a purely relativistic philosophy of cultural multiplicity.

We have seen, in brief, that philosophy arrives at a recognition of the interpretative 'essence' of truth by way of a generalization, above all in contemporary thinking, of the Kantian thematic of the transcendental function of reason, with the vital additional ingredient of the existentialist 'discovery' of the finitude of Dasein. If these theses are not to be presented as a metaphysical discovery of the true objective structure of human existence, on what basis are they to be defended? My earlier reference to Nietzsche's announcement of the death of God already points to what seems the only possible answer to this question: the 'proof' that hermeneutics offers of its own theory is itself a history, both in the sense of *res gestae* and in the sense of *historia rerum gestarum*, and perhaps also in the sense of 'fable' or myth, in that it presents itself as an interpretation (whose claim to validity is such as will even present itself as a competing interpretation that belies it) and not as an objective description of the facts. To carry forward this discourse, sketched here only in outline, one needs to shed light on the fact that neither Kantianism nor, above all, the existentialist discovery of the finiteness of the horizons within which the experience of truth is constituted, can be separated from that series of events which in Nietzschean terms is called the history of nihilism, or else simply modernity. It is all too easy to object that seeking to 'prove' hermeneutics by an appeal to evidence as broad, general and vague as the nihilistic history of modernity risks having no persuasive value whatsoever, given the generic character of the ideas in play. In reply, I will just say that the appeal to modernity, or to the (same) history of nihilism, is no more vague or arbitrary than, let's say, the empiricist reference to immediate experience; or the phenomenological reference to the *Lebenswelt*:

or even than grounding the meaning of propositions on facts about atomic structure gathered by the senses. On the contrary, one could argue for the philosophical validity of hermeneutics alongside other philosophies by showing that all these kinds of supposedly direct evidence do no more than neglect, set hurriedly aside or fail to address with sufficient radicality their own 'historicity' and therefore their own links with the history of nihilism and that of modernity. It is true up to a point that all philosophies, if not explicitly 'ontologies of actuality' (which is, however, probably the case at least for post-Hegelian philosophies, as Habermas has observed[9]), are always responses to contingent questions. Thus, for example, Kantian transcendental philosophy was born as a response on the one hand to the need to secure a foundation for the universal validity of knowledge matured in the course of the modern scientific revolution, and on the other hand to the need for a defence of the 'reasons of the soul' no less profoundly linked to this same scientific revolution. Or again, the origins of hermeneutics, as Dilthey has shown, are profoundly linked to religious, social and political problems arising from the Protestant Reformation. Finally, twentieth-century existentialism and the crisis of neo-Kantianism are not intelligible outside of the historical frame characterized by the earliest signs of mass society (already detected by Nietzsche in the second of the *Untimely Meditations*, and earlier still in Kierkegaard's individualism), the birth of cultural anthropology and the crisis in the foundation of the sciences. Can we take all these (limited and rough) examples of the historico-cultural links of philosophy as chance points of convergence that have made possible the discovery of permanent structural truths? From the point of view of hermeneutics, on account of that within it which is irreducible to metaphysics understood as a universally valid description of permanent structures, one cannot see things in these terms. Hermeneutics, if it wishes to be consistent with its own rejection of metaphysics, cannot but present itself as the most persuasive philosophical interpretation of a situation or 'epoch', and thereby, necessarily, of a provenance. Unable to offer any structural evidence in order to justify itself rationally, it can argue for its own validity only on the basis of a process that, in its view, 'logically' prepares a certain outcome. In this sense, hermeneutics presents itself as a philosophy of modernity (in both subjective and objective senses of the genitive) and even professes to be *the* philosophy of modernity; its truth may be wholly summed up in the claim to be the most persuasive philosophical interpretation of that course of events of which it feels itself to be the outcome. Historicism, then? Yes, if one means that the only valid form of argument in favour of the truth of hermeneutics is a certain interpretation of the events of modernity – for which one must then assume responsibility, both against other competing interpretations and against the historiographical objectivism that mistrusts all such epochal categories while yet taking for granted a naively objectivistic conception of historiography (the events of modernity are so varied and manifold that one cannot speak of them in such general terms) and referring everything to one specialism or another, beginning with its own, which is itself accepted as beyond dispute. Not a deterministic historicism, though. The arguments that hermeneutics offers to support its own interpretation of modernity are aware of being 'only' interpretations; not because they believe there exists outside of themselves a true reality that could be read otherwise, but rather because they admit to being unable to appeal, in support of their own validity, to any immediate objective evidence whatsoever. Their value lies in being able to establish a coherent picture we can share while waiting for others to propose a more plausible alternative.

However, it seems that all this has still not led us to the nihilistic vocation of hermeneutics that, in our hypothesis, was to provide the basis for a more precise and distinctive delineation of the consequences for the traditional problems of philosophy. Yet if one reflects on what the 'hermeneutic' outcome of modernity (which hermeneutics must take on board as an indispensable condition for its own 'truth') signifies for the most traditional problem of philosophy, that of the meaning of Being, the connection between the philosophy of interpretation and nihilism (in the sense the term has in Nietzsche and also beyond) is hard to deny. What becomes of Being in a thinking aware that it cannot identify truth with the objectivity of objects established by (allegedly) direct experience or by positive-scientific method? In the first place, one will at the very least have to speak of Being not in terms of an object or state of affairs, but in terms of 'event', as

Heidegger says. Indeed, according to Derrida – whose premisses, and perhaps this explains his position, are more phenomenological than onticologico-existential – one must no longer speak of Being at all. I shall not discuss this view at length here.[10] The point is that the decision to stop speaking of Being seems to imply an unconscious metaphysical claim; as if one were to read the Nietzschean announcement of the death of God as on a plane with an announcement of his non-existence. No longer speaking of Being is justified either as the attitude that corresponds best to a 'reality' that excludes it and in which there is no Being, or as the recognition of the fulfilment of Being in the history of our culture. But then this history must be told, it is the very history of nihilism as the provenance of hermeneutics and as its private guiding thread for the 'solution' of the traditional problems of philosophy. In the absence of this story, the unconscious metaphysical presupposition stays in place. It is this unconscious, implicit, unintentional metaphysical presupposition that explains the appearance of relativistic irrationalism that some critics detect in Derrida's deconstructionism. If it is not the story of the history of (the dissolution of) Being, deconstruction seems to be an ensemble of conceptual *performances* [in English in the original] entrusted to the sheer artistic flair [*genialità*] of the deconstructor.

If our hypothesis stands, hermeneutics is legitimated as a narrative of modernity, that is, of its own provenance; and moreover it is also, indeed above all, a narrative of the meaning of Being. Not only because it is in connection with the reintroduction of this theme in Heidegger that the basis of the contemporary philosophy of interpretation is laid. It is not by chance that today's hermeneutic philosophy is born in Heidegger, the philosopher whose stated intention was to rethink the meaning of Being, or at least the question of its oblivion. Before Heidegger, as we have already observed, Nietzsche had placed the theory of interpretation and nihilism in relation with one another. For Nietzsche, nihilism signified the 'devaluation of the highest values' and the real world's becoming a fable. There are no facts, only interpretations; and this too is an interpretation. But in what sense should one speak of nihilism in relation to Heideggerian hermeneutics? Without offering a systematic reconstruction here (in part I have carried this out elsewhere,[11] and in part it remains to be done), I will simply draw attention to a few points in order to clarify this thesis. It is worth noting, however, that this thesis is not widely shared in the current Heideggerian literature. It is rather the characteristic theme of what I propose to call the Heideggerian left: not primarily in a political sense, obviously, but in a sense that alludes to the use of the terms right and left in the Hegelian school. Right, in the case of Heidegger, denotes an interpretation of his overcoming of metaphysics as an effort, in spite of everything, somehow to prepare a 'return of Being', perhaps in the form of an apophasic, negative, mystical ontology; left denotes the reading that I propose of the history of Being as the story of a 'long goodbye', of an interminable weakening of Being. In this case, the overcoming of Being is understood only as a recollection of the oblivion of Being, never as making Being present again, not even as a term that always lies beyond every formulation. The reasons for preferring the leftist reading of Heidegger – a reading, moreover, which he himself did not choose – may be summed up by the intention to remain faithful, even beyond the letter of his texts, to the ontological difference, that is, to avoiding the identification of Being with a being. Now, if one thinks, following the rightist interpretation, that Being can 'return' to speak to us beyond the oblivion into which it had fallen, or if one believes that it continues always to elude us just because it transcends the capacity of our intellect and our language, as in the case of apophasic theology – in all these cases it seems that one continues to identify Being with a being. The importance attributed by Heidegger to the notion of, and the very expression, 'metaphysics as the history of Being' points rather in the direction of a conception of Being in which the ontological difference arises precisely in the giving of Being as suspension and withdrawal. Not for nothing is the supreme oblivion of Being that according to which it is thought as presence. It is not a matter, therefore, of remembering Being by making it present again or by hoping for it to make itself present again, but of remembering the oblivion; in our terms, of recognizing the link between the interpretative essence of truth and nihilism. Naturally, not even nihilism must be understood metaphysically, as it would be were one to think of it as a story in which, ultimately, in an nth version of presence as the presence of nothing, Being *is no longer*. And, in the end, nihilism too is an interpretation, and not a description, of a state of things.

In truth, to conclude at least provisionally this first approach to our theme, if we concede that truth is interpretation, that each confirmation or falsification of a proposition can occur only within the horizon of a prior opening, not transcendental but inherited, must we 'logically' proceed to the point of nihilism? The transition is that illustrated by Heidegger's entire body of work – yet which in the vague hermeneutic *koiné* that character-ized our point of departure is clearly not negated, but simply often not fully thematized and elaborated. If one can speak of Being (and one must, in order not to fall unwittingly back into objectiv-isitic metaphysics), it must be sought at the level of those inherited openings (Heidegger also says: in language, which is the house of Being), within which Dasein, man, is always already thrown as into its provenance. This, above all, is the 'nihilistic' meaning of hermeneutics. If we do not think that the transition from the metaphysics of presence to the ontology of provenance is an error, but the event of Being itself, the indication of a 'destiny', then the tendency to weakening – which is, to be sure, only such on the basis of the metaphysical category of presence, of fullness – that this course manifests is the truth of Nietzsche's nihilism, the very meaning of the death of God, of the dissolution of truth as incontrovertible and 'objective' clearness; until now philosophers have seen fit to describe the world, now the moment has arrived to interpret it.

2

Science

To regard hermeneutics as a philosophy that cor-responds (positively as the 'logical' outcome, and not just as a polemical counterpoint) to the becoming of nihilism and thereby of modernity means above all distancing oneself from the attitude that hermeneutic thinkers have so far held towards the positive sciences, the *Naturwissenschaften*. In fact, its vocation for nihilism having been acknowledged, to open this survey of the consequences of hermeneutics with the question of its conception of the natural sciences is already to initiate this change. The decision is by no means a neutral one, dictated solely by the desire to take a broad view of the traditional questions of philosophy from the perspective of hermeneutics. True, at first sight, all one is doing is reviving the problematic of the difference between the *Natur-* and *Geisteswissenschaften* that marked the historicism of the late nineteenth century to which contemporary hermeneutics is linked. But this hermeneutics has itself ever more firmly refused to reconsider that distinction (on the basis of the argument that it was still inspired, in Dilthey, by a submission before the methodological model of the natural sciences), putting it aside in favour of a theory of interpretation constructed primarily in reference to aesthetic experience. Of all the ways in which truth occurs or, as we might say, of all the different types of inaugural event of Being described by Heidegger in an important passage from 'The Origin of the Work of Art', to which he never returned, there is none

that could be identified with the birth of a new scientific hypothesis (for example, the Copernican revolution). In addition to
'setting itself in the work', the text includes amongst the ways that
truth occurs: 'the act that founds a political state . . . the nearness
of that which is not simply a being, but the being that is most of
all . . . the essential sacrifice . . . the thinker's questioning, which,
as the thinking of Being, names Being in its question-worthiness.'[1]
Yet in the following lines it goes on to say explicitly that 'science
is not an original happening of truth, but always the cultivation
of a domain of truth already opened' (cf. also the Addendum at
the end of the essay), more or less the same point as Heidegger
makes in *What is Called Thinking?* where he writes that the
sciences 'are not thinking'.[2] And when Gadamer dedicates the first
part of *Truth and Method* to the retrieval of the experience of the
truth of art he does nothing more, at least from this point of view,
than follow the lead given by Heidegger who, from all the ways
in which the essay from *Holzwege* describes truth as occurring,
and which did not include science, in fact went on to consider, in
all his works, only art and poetry. For hermeneutics, as we have
recalled, truth is not primarily the conformity of statement to
thing, but the opening within which every conformity or deformity
can come about. The opening is not a stable, transcendental
structure of reason, but a legacy, the finite-historical thrownness,
Schickung, destiny, provenance of conditions of possibility that
Heidegger sees incarnated in the historical conditions of natural
languages. The occurrence of the historico-linguistic openings that
make possible the experience of truth as the verification of
statements is given in poetry and, more problematically, in art in
general. In theory, it is also given in other 'ways', listed by
Heidegger in the text cited, but to which, after the essay of 1936,
he never returned.

This Heideggerian legacy marks subsequent hermeneutics in a
decisive way, and is probably responsible not only for its prevailing attitude towards the positive sciences, to the limits of which I
shall return shortly, but ultimately perhaps also for the lack of
recognition of what I have proposed to call the nihilistic vocation
of the philosophy of interpretation. By this I mean that, drawing
primarily on aesthetic experience, hermeneutics further advances
the polemical assertion of the superiority of the human sciences to

the natural sciences found throughout the humanist tradition of philosophy; and in so doing, it closes off the path to a recognition of its own nihilistic vocation, remaining moreover linked to a vision of science and of aesthetic experience itself that is still metaphysical.

Let.us try to clarify this ensemble of transitions. Science does not think, according to Heidegger and Gadamer (but it would be hard to find an explicitly different position in other hermeneuticians such as Ricoeur or Pareyson), because it is not an originary site of the occurrence of truth. Truth as the opening of the horizons within which all that is true or false in the propositional sense can be given has nonetheless always already occurred, given that our every act and conscious thought is made possible by it; yet not being a transcendental structure (for the reasons already noted, that is it is not stable and given once and for all, like the objects it makes accessible), nor ahistorical, it is something that occurs, though not on account of a deliberate act. The model for this occurrence is the creation of the work of art, which the tradition, at least in modernity, is united in regarding as radical newness, and for which reason it speaks of genius and of inspiration by 'nature'. But if one does not wish to hark back to the Romantic tradition, an example of what Heidegger has in mind when speaking of the occurrence of truth can also be seen in Kuhnian paradigms, which seem to be far more manageable 'objects', even for someone unwilling to re-adopt a romantic position. It is hard to say (though I tend to believe it myself) whether Kuhnian paradigms, which are not 'instituted' on the basis of a correction of the errors of the preceding paradigm, are not themselves inspired by, or at least assimilable to, the Romantic aesthetic of the genius, or even the Heideggerian conception of the openings of truth. Testimony in favour of the latter hypothesis may be found in the distinction, put forward by Rorty in *Philosophy and the Mirror of Nature*,[3] between hermeneutics and epistemology, where epistemology denotes that thought which moves within existing and accepted paradigms, doing what Kuhn calls 'normal science' (that is, it solves problems according to the rules of the existing paradigm), whereas hermeneutics is the encounter with a new paradigm – an encounter that in Rorty is very similar (or simply identical) in character to the experience of art as the opening of truth described by Heidegger and Gadamer. Rorty rejects the Diltheyan distinction between the natural and human sciences, and does not explicitly rule out the possibility that a 'hermeneutic' encounter with a new paradigm might occur even within the domain of the positive sciences; thus his aesthetic model does not lead to the humanistic consequences that by contrast we see in Gadamer. Nonetheless, it remains unclear whether the encounter with a new paradigm may truly be thought of as 'scientific work', for such work seems to imply an active presentation and solution of problems that places it firmly on the side of epistemology. Yet this is the reason why Heidegger and Gadamer believe that science 'does not think': given its characteristic attention to methodological procedures, the only possible form it can take seems to be that of normal science, whereas a revolutionary science would be difficult to distinguish from poetic creation. More recently, Rorty has spoken of 'redescriptions' in order to indicate something like the institution of new paradigms (new systems of metaphors for describing the world) in terms that are substantially aesthetic.[4] Even the sense that Popper attributed to metaphysics as a pointer towards new paths for science could perhaps align itself with a view like this.[5]

Evidently, in spite of Rorty's explicit rejection of the traditional distinction between the human and natural sciences, he too regards hermeneutics as ultimately characterized by way of an aesthetic model. Not even humanism's recognition of the superiority of the human sciences is foreign to Rorty: for if, as he explicitly observes, what is important for him is that the 'conversation continue', then the redescriptions – poetic creations, new paradigms – are what give existence meaning, and from his perspective philosophers and poets, or scientific revolutionaries (but how can one tell them apart?) end up appearing more vitally important than those who resolve the riddles within existing paradigms.

What follows will clarify the sense in which the privilege given by hermeneutics to aesthetic experience and the consequent, often merely implicit, devaluation of the natural sciences vis-à-vis the human sciences coincides with (or is perhaps at once the cause and consequence of) an incapacity to grasp the nihilistic meaning of the philosophy of interpretation.

It seems in fact that hermeneutics, even now, is exclusively concerned with relating the work of scientific specialists and their complex categorial structures back to the *Lebenswelt*, to the pre-categorial lifeworld within which, above all, the new openings of truth occur in historico-natural language ... This, ultimately, is one of the senses of hermeneutics as *koiné*; and in fact it is here on this terrain that it meets Rortian pragmatism and far more generally speaking the tradition of linguistic analysis inaugurated by the later Wittgenstein, the theory of communicative action, communitarianism, the multiculturalism of the anthropologists, and above all the various legacies of phenomenology and existentialism. Hermeneutics has probably been able to establish itself as the *koiné* only because philosophical movements of the last few decades have registered renewed interest in the motivations behind existentialism, phenomenology and early twentieth-century *Kulturkritik* in general, which have themselves now achieved a fresh relevance of their own by virtue of the growing intensity of the problems posed by the relation, in brief, between science and society. Does the popularity enjoyed, roughly since the end of the sixties (but this needs clarification), by an expression such as 'the community of researchers' have anything to do with the rediscovery of the work of Peirce,[6] or indeed more directly with the 'sociological' circumstances of American scientific research which was, during the years of the Vietnam war, deeply involved with military commissions? This argument could, I believe, be used to explain the attention received by a work like that of Thomas Kuhn, which corresponds to a more pronounced, if not completely new, awareness of the 'historicity' of science.[7] Again, these observations confirm that, as I have suggested, the concern with drawing the domain of science's categorial exposition back to the lifeworld is, also in the ethico-political sense, one of the good reasons that underpin the privilege accorded by hermeneutics to the human sciences: the fate of democracy is at stake here. Since only if there is a rationality of the *Lebenswelt* that can draw back to itself, interpret and up to a point unify the plurality of languages, ends and autonomous value systems that support the scientific and technical worlds, will a society be possible that is not given over entirely to the power of specialists and technicians, and in which citizens may have the last word in major collective decisions.

In any case, and aside from all these good ethico-political reasons, what I intend to propose is that if hermeneutics is presented in these terms as an up-to-date version – in a sense less idealistic, Kantian or transcendentalist than linguistic and communicative – of the phenomenological problematic of the *Lebenswelt*, it risks betraying its own premises, or at least not developing them to their fullest theoretical potential, and may ultimately struggle to differentiate itself from a general and often relativistic philosophy of culture.

It seems that hermeneutics can avoid this risk by adopting the strong and normative sense attributed to the concept of *Lebenswelt*, lifeworld, by Habermas in the *Theory of Communicative Action*. A lifeworld is the entire shared culture, lived in everyday communication, that must serve as the background to the various types of 'special' action that make up the life of a society, and by this is meant strategic action (which comprises science), action according to norms and expressive action. But by what right does the lifeworld as a whole stake its claim as the normative horizon within which each domain of social action must find its place – without any undue 'colonization' of one by another or above all of the lifeworld as a whole? The normative significance of this idea (as I have argued elsewhere[8]) seems to depend wholly on the fact that the discursive and dialogical character of the lifeworld – as the supporting horizon of a culture – is in fact specific to Western culture, and perhaps even to the 'transparent' community of modern scientists alone. There would be nothing wrong with this, if Habermas had explicitly thematized the teleology implicit in this aspect of his theory, as in fact Husserl did when, in the *Crisis*, he maintained that the rationality which first appeared in Greece, and which dominated the evolution of European culture, is a guiding value that holds for the whole of humanity;[9] however, for a number of good reasons, Habermas does not subscribe to any such rationalist historicism – which, moreover, phenomenology too would find problematic.

Habermas, it will rightly be said, is hardly a 'classic' example of hermeneutic philosophy.[10] Yet analogous problems arise even for a hermeneutic author like Gadamer, at least in the absence of an ontological radicalization, relating to the 'history of Being', of certain suggestions that, while present in his work, he declines fully to develop. What Habermas today calls the 'lifeworld' was, in *Truth and Method* and in subsequent works by Gadamer (see *Reason in the Age of Science*[11]), the *logos* as a shared rationality which exists in the natural language of a community and which is made up of a vocabulary, a grammar and above all a textual tradition bearing the contents that come to establish the original opening of truth within which the community lives. Whereas Habermas staves off relativism from his lifeworld by attributing to it, albeit rather surreptitiously, a transcendental and normative structure that is in fact modelled on Western modernity, Gadamer avoids this metaphysical trap, without falling back into relativism, by theorizing the indefinite opening of historical horizons, their unlimited susceptibility to interpretation. One thereby arrives at an implicit 'humanist' conclusion: the task of thinking, if one is not to remain bound by the terms of specialist languages and factional values (with all that this implies, not least from the ethico-political point of view), is not only that of drawing the particular languages back to the *logos*-language of the community and harmonizing them with it (above all, ethically), but also that of broadening the horizon of the lifeworld to discover an ever greater number of links with other worlds and cultures, with which it is in principle always able to communicate – this primarily, of course, with cultural worlds from which, albeit distantly, the lifeworld arises by way of a deep association with the literary, artistic and philosophical tradition.

Although distinct, Gadamer's position raises the same questions as those presented by the normative import of the idea of the lifeworld in Habermas. In both cases the need arises for a more explicit historicity. In Habermas this need originates with the recognition that the normative features of the lifeworld are linked to the historical becoming of a particular lifeworld, that of Western society, and yet are circulated by way of the transcendental structure of every possible lifeworld. This amounts to saying that Habermas, speaking from within a well-defined tradition, a specific lifeworld, believes he is speaking 'from nowhere', from the usual universal, panoramic or metaphysical point of view. Yet even Gadamer, who has a far more acute awareness of the historicity of every opening of truth, seems to want to treat the tradition as if it were an abstract term within which all 'positions' must obviously lie, but which we refuse to determine in specific terms, thereby refusing to situate ourselves within it.

Does this tradition, which is the living life of the *logos*-language and to which thinking is called to respond by drawing back to it all specialisms, regional values and the many artificial languages in which the social world is articulated, have a meaning beyond its mere globalness? By analogy, one could invoke here a thesis put forward by Karl Mannheim, in *Ideology and Utopia*, at the point where he seems to ground the freedom from ideology that distinguishes the bourgeois intellectual (taking the place here of Lukács's proletariat) on the fact that his essentially historical (historiographist) formation renders him acutely aware of the relativity of all theories:[12] relativism once more, if only as the suspension of full assent to any particular position of thinking whatsoever. Moreover, as I think is shown by a certain theoretical inconclusiveness on the part of phenomenology (from which some, like Enzo Paci, emerge by wedding it to Marxist historicism), the reference to the *Lebenswelt* typically ends up something like this: every categorization is 'suspended' from the lifeworld, whereupon, ultimately, every decision regarding its truth is also suspended (the *epoché* as a definitive attitude?).

I shall not refer here to Heidegger's existentialist 'decisionism', which may well have been in part responsible for his breaking with phenomenology. Instead, I shall draw attention to the fact that, oddly enough, hermeneutics taken simply as an up-to-date version of the *Lebenswelt* thematic typically seems to display all those limitations which, in my view, make of it a philosophy without consequences: the absence of a radicalization of its own historicity, the absence of a recognition of its own nihilistic vocation, the humanist privileging of the human sciences as against the natural sciences. As long as hermeneutics continues to support the humanist case for the superiority of the human sciences over the natural sciences – however well this attitude may be justified by the need to prevent the fragmentation of life into specialisms and the fall of democracy into the hands of experts – it will be unable to accomplish the projected overcoming of metaphysics inscribed in its own beginnings and which constitutes its true originality.

Rather, it is precisely in the recognition of itself as corresponding to a historical situation determined essentially by the experimental natural sciences that hermeneutics rediscovers its own nihilistic vocation. This decisive meaning of the sciences is that in relation to which the existentialist reflection first arises, not only in Heidegger, but also in Husserl's philosophy of the *Lebenswelt* and subsequent phenomenology. Early twentieth-century existentialism, and more generally the whole culture of the historical avant-garde in which is expressed what Bloch, in one of his earliest works, called the 'spirit of utopia',[13] is a response to the world of incipient total organization shaped by the sciences and the technologies they made possible. The reduction of the categorial to the *Lebenswelt*, which is still the sense of the hermeneutic *koiné* today, and for which, as I have repeatedly underlined, there are good reasons, remains, however, bound to this moment of the history of twentieth-century culture. Even the demonization of the mass media – the high point of the technologization of the world – by Adorno and the Frankfurt school in general is only a variant of the spiritual attitude marked by the *Kulturkritik* of the beginning of the century. However, this attitude remains no more than a humanist response to modern techno-science inspired by a philosophy that, while it has seen the limits of metaphysical objectivism (which thinks Being on the model of beings and thus on the model of the object verified experimentally by science and at once manipulated and manipulable by technology), does not manage to see clearly that the overcoming of metaphysics requires a more radical recognition of its own historicity. Science and technology are, from this point of view, contingent 'contents' of a horizon that opens in the natural *logos*-language of historic humanities. But this *logos* is still treated as a stable structure, precisely as the 'lifeworld', or at least in terms of a generic historicity that seems simply to coincide with the 'constitutive' finitude of human existence.[14]

It is from Heidegger and the transition from the first to the second phase of his philosophy that we learn in which direction a thinking more decisively committed to the recognition of its own historically qualified character can and must move. This transition is for example evident in the fact that, whereas in *Being and Time* 'the' world is still in every instance phrased in the singular (man is Dasein, and thereby Being-in-the-world), in the essay 'The

Origin of the Work of Art' (1936) it becomes 'a' world. In the entire second phase of his work (which is not a reversal of the premises of Being and Time, but their development in a direction only glimpsed in that book), Heidegger strives to understand not the (objective, metaphysical) structures of existence, but the meaning (of the history) of Being, as it is determined in the completed epoch of metaphysics that is modernity, the age of science and technology. Once the transition from the world as a common structure of Dasein to worlds as historical openings of Being has been accomplished, the premises of a different attitude towards science are also set forth: no longer (only) a defence of the Lebenswelt against colonization by specialist branches of knowledge and the applications of technology, but an attentiveness to the transformations that science and technology, as determinant factors in modernity, 'bring' to the meaning of Being. What I said earlier about hermeneutics (in the first chapter), namely that it can 'be proven' only insofar as it cor-responds to modernity, is wholly applicable to Heidegger's ultra-metaphysical thinking. It is above all in his eyes that the legitimation of the truth of a theory cannot be sought in the evidence of a ground, of a stable structure. If a post-metaphysical thinking is at all possible, for Heidegger, it can only have its source in a different occurrence than Being itself; and the history of Being in modernity is, above all, a history of techno-science. It is against this background that the passage from Identity and Difference on the 'first oppressing flash of Ereignis' in the world of the Ge-Stell makes sense.[15] And this is the meaning of an essay like 'The Age of the World Picture',[16] which is, I believe, always wrongly taken to be nothing more than the expression of a humanist, anti-scientific and, in the final analysis, anti-modern position. Here we come across the alternative between what I have called left and right Heideggerianism. While the rightist reading may well prevail in Heidegger's self-understanding, it does not encompass texts such as those cited above which point out a different path, one in line with the overall sense of his polemic against metaphysics as the thinking of presence. This other path – opened but not actually travelled by Heidegger – can (and must, in my view) be followed, accepting all the attendant risks and responsibilities. For at its end lies a consideration of modern science as the principal agent in a nihilistic transformation of the meaning of Being; that is, as a positive step towards a world in which there are no facts, only interpretations. In 'The Age of the World Picture', however, in contrast to the hermeneutic privileging of the human sciences it is significant that Heidegger situates even these sciences entirely in the general category of planned and 'consolidating' research that dominates modern techno-scientific knowledge. In science as research planned and industriously applied to single regions of beings, metaphysics is articulated in its most complete form: the world must be drawn back to a general system of causes and effects, to a potentially totalizing image that the scientific subject always has at her or his disposal. The being that has become an object of representation 'incurs in a certain manner a loss of Being'.[17] All this happens not only, in overly abstract terms, because it is in modernity that metaphysics – the thinking of objectification – unfolds its originary essence (already fully present in the Platonic doctrine of ideas as the representable structure of Being); this accomplishment occurs (although it is probably not a matter of a distinct origin: Heidegger does not think of Christianity as an event external to the history of metaphysics) by way of the liberation of modern man from divine authority, which Heidegger pictures for the most part according to the current historiographical models (including Hegel's *Phenomenology*). The reduction of the world to images, to a system of 'serviceable' causal links, is not only a matter of theoretical reason. It is a way of assuring oneself of reality and of one's own fate within it. And when man rebels against divine authority, the practical essence of representation itself becomes more explicit and the assurance must become absolute. The will to power that sustains the objectifying thought of metaphysics becomes more explicit in modernity, partly as a result of secularization. However, this is a decisive step on the path of nihilism. For in becoming representation, as we have already seen, the being loses its Being 'in a certain manner'. But this loss becomes radical when the image of the world, openly displaying its practical dominative character, multiplies into contrasting images in conflict with each other. It is this conflict that sets in train a massive enlargement of the systems of calculation and prediction, to the point where this movement to the extremes of calculability leads to a general incalculability: the

age of the world picture gives way to the dissolution of this image
in a Babel of conflicting images; and '[w]ith this struggle of world
views the modern age first enters into the part of its history that is
the most decisive and probably the most capable of enduring'.[18]
Heidegger's text is strewn with indications that keep us from
reading this description of modernity (only) as a long invective
and an invitation to a hypothetical conversion. The incalculability
casts a sort of shadow over all things, the shadow of the loss of
Being. 'In truth, however, the shadow is a manifest, though
inpenetrable, testimony to the concealed emitting of light.'[19] 'This
shadow, however, points to something else, which it is denied to
us today to know.'[20]

The relation of hermeneutics to modern techno-science breaks
with all metaphysical and humanist associations when hermeneutics, taking science seriously as a determinant factor in the
configuration of Being in modernity, grasps the essential nihilistic
meaning of science which is at the same time constitutive of its
own destiny. The world as a conflict of interpretations and
nothing more is not an image of the world that has to be defended
against the realism and positivism of science. It is modern science,
heir and completion of metaphysics, that turns the world into a
place where there are no (longer) facts, only interpretations. It is
not a matter, for hermeneutics, of setting limits to scientism, of
resisting the triumph of science and technology in the name of a
humanist culture, of standing up for the 'lifeworld' against
calculation, planning and total organization. The critique that
hermeneutics can and must move against the techno-scientific
world is aimed, if anything, to aid it in a recognition of its own
nihilistic meaning and to take it up as a guiding thread for
judgements, choices and the orientation of individual and collective life. What, if not nihilism and the dissolution of the 'principle
of reality', is the approach of science to situations in which the
idea of proving a scientific hypothesis as the apprehension of a
fact accessible to the senses is no longer intelligible? When the
scientist verifies that the pointers of two machines coincide, or
that the calculation of one computer 'confirms' that of another,
are we still dealing with a lived experience, with something
Husserl in his *Crisis in the European Sciences* would call *lebens-
weltlich*?[21] Technicians guided by science have transformed the

world of objects into a system in which it is increasingly difficult to distinguish the satisfaction of natural 'needs' from the superfluous response to induced desires; and is this not another sign of the corrosive effect that science and technology exerts on every 'principle of reality'?

If hermeneutics takes its own anti-metaphysical orientation and nihilistic vocation seriously and encourages us to read modernity in this sense, it will undoubtedly appear far more problematic and less neutral than its emergence as a *koiné* led us to believe; but it will be able to make a less vague contribution to the understanding of what in truth, as Heidegger would say, remains to-be-thought.

3

Ethics

Recognizing the nihilistic implications of hermeneutics seems to liberate us from the generality of a philosophy of culture that continually oscillates between relativism and transcendentalist metaphysics (depending on whether one identifies the horizon of interpretation with the lifeworld understood as a particular culture or as a universal normative reference point). But it also opens the way to a conception of the world as a conflict of interpretations that seems dangerously close to the Nietzschean celebration of the will to power. What the nihilist ontology of hermeneutics provokes, we might say, is not so much theoretical opposition as legitimate ethical concern. Yet, given that the world is plainly nothing more than a conflict of interpretations, is it still possible for interpretations to emerge that are so compelling as to precipitate violence and struggle in the current sense of the word? If we allow ourselves to follow the thread of nihilism that we seem to have picked out as the overarching sense of hermeneutics, it will be hard not to concede that making the interpretative essence of all truth explicit entails a profound modification in the kind of practical relation one has to what is true. The interpretations that lead to violent struggle are those that do not recognize themselves as such – and which, as in the tradition, regard other interpretations simply as fraudulent and wrong. Even Nietzsche, the philosopher of the will to power, saw this. In a famous note on 'European nihilism' from the summer of 1887, he mused that

when, in the world of nihilism, the fight between the 'weak' and
the 'strong' is laid bare in its elements and no longer masked by
metaphysical and consolatory lies, it is the moderate that are
ultimately destined to triumph, 'those who do not require any
extreme articles of faith; those who not only concede but love a
fair amount of accidents and nonsense'.[1] Leaving aside the philological problems raised by the will to power in Nietzsche, its
ambiguity lies above all in the difficulty of squaring it with
nihilism, another of the great 'key-words' of the mature Nietzsche.
It is perhaps not by chance that he speaks a great deal in the notes
from his final period of the will to power as art, and of the artist
as one who experiments and in so doing transcends the interests
tied to the struggle for existence: a figure far distant from the
strong subject that many interpreters – basing their readings on
other texts by Nietzsche – have wished to identify with the
übermensch. There is no strict relation between nihilism and
violence. In fact, even if one cannot attribute this to Nietzsche,
one of the effects of nihilism may well be to undermine the reasons
by which violence is justified and nourished. And if one considers
the original motives behind the Heideggerian 'revolution' against
metaphysics (which takes up many components of the artistic and
philosophical avant-garde of the early twentieth century, welding
them into a philosophically rigorous and productive system), one
can justifiably claim that they are ethical (or ethico-political) in
character rather than theoretical, and that they reject metaphysics
– the thinking of Being as presence and objectivity – insofar as
they see it above all as a violent thinking. It would in fact be hard
to imagine that Heidegger, in posing the problem of the meaning
of Being afresh in *Being and Time*, was seeking a truer and more
adequate representation of Being than that inherited from metaphysics. One must not forget that, although the distance from
metaphysics is developed above all in his later works, the critique
of the idea of truth as the conformity of a proposition to how
things are, and thus of each truth as an adequate description of a
given, is already clearly formulated in *Being and Time*. But if one
cannot refer back to the demand for a more objectively adequate
conception, the need to rethink the meaning of Being might
reasonably be explained as an expression of the existentialist
mood of the early twentieth century. The theoretical motivation

of existentialism (Kierkegaard's intolerance of Hegelian rationalism, the revolt of the philosophy of life against positivistic science)
reflected above all diffidence for what had begun, especially in
the war years, to emerge as a world of total organization (as
Adorno would later describe it) and which seemed as though it
were a kind of fully realized metaphysical system. For Heidegger,
such a world represented the triumph of the objectifying and
calculating attitude as an expression of the metaphysical tendency
to identify Being with what is present and controllable. In
consequence either human existence becomes unthinkable in terms
of Being, or it too must be reduced to pure presence, calculability
and manipulability.

Hermeneutics, born out of Heidegger's polemic against metaphysics, remains to this day a thinking motivated primarily by
ethical considerations. After Heidegger, and with points of departure that are different from his without being too far removed
from them, Levinas and Adorno have also taught us to mistrust
metaphysics, in view less of its theoretical failings than of its
violence; either because, as Adorno thinks, its overriding interest
in essences and the universal inclines it to accept, in the name of
the universal, that individuals be trampled underfoot; or because,
as Levinas thinks, the demand that Being be grasped as the
condition for encountering the single existent opens the way to
the same aberrations. However, it is perhaps to Heidegger's
rejection of simple presence as the essential character of Being
that one must above all refer, both to ground the rejection of
metaphysics (given that there is some doubt as to whether
Adorno's and Levinas' reasons truly hold – the thought of the
universal has not always and necessarily given way to violence
and oppression), and for a definition of the violence in terms that
do not themselves repeat metaphysics in their turn.[2] Of a piece
with the 'ethical' motivations that can and must be attributed to
the Heidegger of *Being and Time*, the subsequent Heideggerian
theory of metaphysics as the oblivion of Being and the identification of Being with the givenness of the object in the incontrovertibility of presence can legitimately be read as the most distinctive
philosophical outcome of the twentieth-century rejection of metaphysics as a thinking of violence. It is not because the universal
necessarily leads to the violation of the rights of the individual

that metaphysics must be overcome; indeed, the metaphysicians themselves are in a good position to say that the very rights of the individual have often been defended precisely in the name of metaphysical grounds – for example in the doctrine of natural right. Rather, it is as a thinking of the incontrovertible presence of Being – as the ultimate foundation before which one can only fall silent and, perhaps, feel admiration – that metaphysics is a violent thinking: the foundation, if it is given in incontrovertible evidence that no longer admits further enquiry, is like an authority that keeps things quiet and takes control without explanation. It is here that we find the root of the inclination of metaphysics to that type of violence against the individual that so often accompanies it and that so preoccupied Adorno and Levinas. I believe (and one could try to demonstrate this with a more detailed discussion of the idea of violence in the history of thinking) that the suppressive authority of the foundation given 'in presence' may be the only possible way to define violence without recourse to metaphysical ideas like essence, nature and the structure of Being.

That thinking foundations – metaphysical foundationalism – is indeed a violent thinking is not an objective 'given' that may itself be proved beyond doubt (thereby contradicting itself). It is what 'emerges' from the narration-interpretation of the history of metaphysics, which brings us to the implications noted by Adorno and Levinas, Heidegger's vision of metaphysics as the premiss from which scientism and the total organization of society logically follow, and the Nietzschean idea according to which foundational thinking is a kind of excessive reaction to a state of insecurity that is no longer ours.[3]

If these are the ethical demands that inspire hermeneutics in its original form in Heidegger, not only in part but comprehensively, how does the philosophy of interpretation of today cor-respond? And according to our hypothesis here, what difference does a more open acknowledgement of the nihilistic implications make? I shall show that, above all in this domain of ethics, the acknowledgement of the nihilistic vocation of ethics is decisive in ridding hermeneutics of the vagueness with which it is increasingly associated, and which reveals its 'fall back' into metaphysics.

We have already seen the ethical positions linked to hermeneutics, both by their authors and by current opinion, begin to take shape in the preceding discussion of the relation between hermeneutics and the experimental sciences of nature. This is probably not accidental: insofar as it is not a metaphysical theory of imperatives deduced from structures and essences, but interpretation itself, and thus a response to an historico-destinal giving of Being, a hermeneutic ethics will have above all to address that region of existence which, here today, decisively determines the man–Being relation: namely, science and modern technology. A hermeneutic ethics, if such a thing exists, will therefore be nothing other than a response of thinking to the man-Being relation as it is configured in the epoch of completed metaphysics, that is, in the epoch of the world picture.

The ethical responses put forward in the hermeneutic *koiné* to the modern configuration of the man–Being relation may be characterized in three ways; there is an ethics of communication, an ethics of redescription and an ethics of continuity. With the first we associate the names of Habermas and Apel, with the second the name of Rorty and with the third that of Gadamer.

The names of Apel and Habermas make it immediately clear what is meant by an ethics of communication; above all for Apel, it is clear that the experience of truth is conditioned by our relation to a language that is at once the medium in which we work and that in which we ourselves exist.[4] Whatever its historical particularity may be, every language carries within it a kind of ineluctable vocation for communication. In this regard, Apel cites Wittgenstein and his idea that 'one cannot play a language game by oneself' since even the most arbitrary of private languages requires the user to double up, acting first as one who invents the rules and then as one who follows them.[5] But this implies that the one who observes the rules is responsible for this observance: and the responsibility is a responsibility to someone else, to the ideal interlocutor who, even if only as the selfsame subject taken as the institutor of rules, features in every instance of language use. To précis Apel, there can be no experience of the world without the use of language, and every use of language (excepting the most extreme performative contradiction) implies a responsibility to an interlocutor, even if only ideal, to respect the rules of the linguistic game. Accordingly, the recognition of the linguistic-interpretative character of our experience of the world also entails a clear ethical directive; to respect the rights of the interlocutor, which implicitly I cannot fail to recognize as equal to mine as a speaking subject. As we know, on this basis Apel formulates the principle of an unlimited community of communication, to which, by way of a complex but for the most part convincing line of argument, he traces back (in the manner of a Kantian categorical imperative) the fundamental norms of morality (even the duty to avoid war or to further the survival of one's neighbour is referred back to the duty to guarantee the possibility of an 'unlimited' communication, in which interlocutors genuinely have the same rights[6]).

The normative significance of the theory of communicative action developed by Habermas, mentioned above, is couched in similar terms, although with less emphasis on the use of language and a marked concern for the defence of the lifeworld as a milieu that makes possible and sustains the various forms of action. Since all action aspires to its own specific rationality, which is intelligible only in terms of the defence of its validity to other subjects, to act according to reason, and therefore ethically, means to make explicit this implicit 'argumentativity' and, above all, to keep its possibility alive by preserving and developing in the lifeworld the conditions of a communication that is not opaque, that is not impeded by inequalities, ideological obscurantism, deliberate distortions or structures of domination.

The objections that can be put, and that have been put, to this ethics of communication from the point of view of hermeneutics stress its idealistic and therefore subjectivistic and potentially solipsistic implications. Can one cultivate the ideal of an absolute transparency of communication while remaining faithful to the basic conditions, namely the interpretative character, of every experience of truth? The ideal of transparency, of the elimination of every opacity in communication, seems to be perilously close (at least from the theoretical point of view) to the conception of truth as objectivity determined by a 'neutral' subject modelled on the form of 'metaphysical' subjectivity incarnated most recently in the ideal of the modern scientist. Seen in these terms, the theory of communicative action might look like a glaring example of the colonization of the lifeworld by a specific form of action, the scientific-descriptive, surreptitiously adopted as a model. Should preserving the lifeworld in its irreducibility and its function as a sustaining horizon not also mean defending it from the demands of total transparency? It is less a matter of rejecting the practical-political conclusions of Apel's and Habermas's discourse than of asking whether one can share its theoretical bases and above all whether these bases do not turn out to be unduly strengthened by the generally acceptable nature of those conclusions. And then also at the level of the practical-political conclusions, does the idea of a non-opaque communication not imply at least the risk of making necessary a category of experts (perhaps members of a central committee or an ecclesiastical hierarchy) who decide which communications are to be considered distorted or, in the end, what are the true interests of the masses? As far as hermeneutics and the inspiration most proper to it are concerned, the theses of Apel and Habermas (considered here in view of what they have in common) bring us face to face with the problem of deciding whether or not the philosophy of interpretation really does contain the ideal of a totally transparent communication: which, it seems, it does not, if one considers that the whole of hermeneutics after Schleiermacher has if anything been built around an awareness of the impossibility of conceiving the interpretative act as an identification with the object, or more generally the other, to be interpreted.[7]

In Rorty's theory of redescription one finds an almost symmetrical reversal of the ethics of communication.[8] As we have remarked in earlier chapters, Rorty begins from an idea of hermeneutics that, while it does not wholly reject the ideal of an identification with the other to be interpreted (given that the definitive outcome of the hermeneutic encounter is an empathetic sharing of paradigms and forms of life), insists rather on difference. In order that the conversation continue – an aim that does not in fact seem to be grounded in Rorty (unless perhaps in a vitalism) – it is necessary that the partners of the game of communication can reciprocally offer one another not only variations within a shared paradigm, but also and above all proposals for the 'redescription' of oneself and of the world that precisely call for a hermeneutic, and not merely epistemological, approach. While it is true that Rorty is careful not to frame his theory of redescriptions as an ethical proposal, there is nothing in his texts to prohibit this reading.[9] In fact it seems entirely permissible to take it in this way, as one of the paths open to hermeneutics (in its general sense as *koiné)* when it seeks to respond to the question of ethics. Other not insignificant reasons also encourage us to read Rorty's theory like this; the ethics that one can draw from Foucault's mature writings is very similar to the theory of redescriptions: as Deleuze has written, for him 'the struggle for subjectivity manifests itself as the right to difference, variation and metamorphosis'. Moreover, Foucault in all probability offers a fresh reading of the Nietzschean idea of the conflict of interpretations. It seems that to some extent both Rorty and Foucault, like Nietzsche before them, adopt the principle that if in the age of nihilism there is still a duty that we can recognize as coherent, it is not that of respecting the table of existing values, but that of inventing new tables of values, new lifestyles, new systems of metaphors for speaking of the world and of our own experience. In each of these cases, it is as though interpretation were conceived less as a means to understanding than as an activity in which the subjectivity of the interpreter is implicated – to which aspect, moreover, special emphasis should be given. That knowledge of truth is an interpretation means that truth is never neutral, but always distinguished in relation to a historical moment, a personality or a particular individual history. Hermeneutics – as an interpretative activity and as a philosophical theory – must guard against treating these personal aspects of the experience of the true as provisional and accidental moments to be overtaken in the direction of the transparency spoken of by Apel and Habermas. An extreme version of the position expressed today by Rorty may be seen in the idea of 'conspiracy' that Klossowski places at the centre of his reading of Nietzsche.[10] Although tied in the most complex terms to the idea of the eternal return as a selective thought, the Klossowskian conspiracy is a typical aestheticist reading of the ethical consequences of Nietzschean nihilism, whose features may also be distinguished in Rorty's redescriptions. Even so, Klossowski's conspiracy cannot pave the way for an established paradigm and never wishes to do so: it remains a redescription that, insofar as it responds to the selective principle of the eternal return, by definition does not found any stability whatsoever. It preserves the minority character that must, it seems, be attributed to the artistic genius and the 'pure' revolutionary. But even for Rorty, what counts in proposing new redescriptions is ultimately the poetic or revolutionary moment – in Kuhn's sense of revolutionary science – far more than any capacity for founding historical concreteness and continuity.[11]

It is all too easy – although probably also correct, given that it seems to concern two diametrically opposed ways of understanding the meaning of hermeneutics – to observe that if Habermas and Apel placed exclusive emphasis, perhaps moralistically, on transparency as the meaning and objective of interpretation, Rorty (or Klossowski, or Foucault), in connection with his anti-foundationalist formation, exclusively emphasizes the irreducibility of the redescriptions to any kind of continuity.[12] What is valued seems here to be identified with the new, the unheard of, the 'stroke of genius' – precisely the genius of the Romantic tradition; and the more it is aware of its complete unfoundedness and unfoundability, the more highly it is valued (this is why Heidegger and Nietzsche, united by dint of their offering pure redescriptions of themselves and of the world, are 'worth' less than Proust, who, as a Nietzschean expression has it, knows that he is 'only a poet, just a clown'[13]). As with Habermasian and Apelian transcendentalism, here too we have difficulty recognizing the inspiration behind hermeneutics, especially the conviction that interpretation is the articulation of something understood, and thus the response to a call whose source, in Heideggerian terms, lies in the historico-destinal thrownness in which Dasein is located. Neither the 'redescriptions' offered by philosophers like Heidegger and Nietzsche nor those of artists like Proust are really ironical in the way that Rorty imagines. Philosophers claim to 'found' their theses in some way; but the cogency encountered in the work of even the most innovative artists and which sustains the legitimacy of their work and the assertion that it has value for others, is not purely and simply the artists' faith in themselves, a complete and wholly arbitrary assumption of total responsibility.[14] If the still metaphysical, and therefore non-hermeneutic, character of the ethics of unlimited communication manifested itself in the reaffirmation of a transcendental structure of reason – taken from fact and adopted as a norm – here the return to metaphysics is clearly signposted by the recovery, only partially disguised, of a philosophy of the creative genius. To be sure, it is no longer legitimized by somehow having its roots in nature and the mysterious rules of nature, but it is at least implicitly justified by a vitalistic celebration of creativity which remains the only way to explain why it is important that 'the conversation continue'.[15]

The only ethics that appears to be coherent with the antimetaphysical inspiration of hermeneutics is perhaps that formulated in the years following the publication of *Truth and Method* by Hans Georg Gadamer, whose name is moreover linked to a whole movement for the 'rehabilitation of practical philosophy'.[16] The pre-eminence of Gadamer's position among the different ethics inspired by the philosophy of interpretation (or that commonly pass for hermeneutic ethics) is due moreover to the fact that his theory seems able to encompass the motives and demands voiced and unilaterally affirmed in the ethics of communication and in those of redescription. Gadamerian ethics is wholly an affirmation of the value of dialogue, even if it does not believe that dialogue has to be modelled on an ideal of transparency that, in the end, would render it inessential. And as for the novelty of redescriptions, one can say that it is made into a feature of every interpretative act, which as an 'application' to the present situation of the inherited textual legacy (laws, religious messages, works of art, historical documents) constitutes authentic, and the only conceivable (increment in), Being. However, the accent here is placed on continuity. Furthermore, *Truth and Method* defends the truth of the experience of art on the basis of a critique of aestheticism and aesthetic consciousness, whose features can be seen precisely in the discontinuity and the ahistorical temporal singularity so beautifully represented in the figure of Kierkegaard's Don Giovanni. The historicity of the Kierkegaardian ethical stage is in all likelihood the point of reference that most helps one to understand the meaning of Gadamer's hermeneutic ethics. Like Kierkegaard, the author to which Gadamer so clearly refers here is Hegel. The moral task is, for him, to realize something like Hegel's ethical life; the integration of everyone's single experiences into a continuity of individual existence that can only be sustained on the basis of belonging to a historical community which, as we have already said, lives in language. The community, for its part, is not something closed and isolated in a point of space or a moment of history. Like the horizon, it moves with us. In this way, the integration of individual experiences in the horizons that sustain them is never concluded. Interpretative mediation has no limits, any more than the traducibility and commensurability of cultures.

Not only is Gadamer's position the most characteristically hermeneutic in the field of ethics, but he has also contributed more than anyone else to the popularization of hermeneutics and its becoming a *koiné*. For this very reason, and without any polemical intent (indeed, following the path opened by him), it is on the theses of Gadamer that the nihilistic radicalization we wish to propose here must be performed. It is a matter of developing what we have already noted with regard to science and the *Lebenswelt*, adding to this, however, a further consideration; namely, that the idea of a morality as the infinite recomposition of continuity (almost a kind of widening and ever renewed reconstruction of the hermeneutic circle) seems to risk conceiving the authenticity of existence, or the 'good life', or as one might also say, virtue, in terms of perfect integration into a totality that, as such, would be the good. As I have tried to show more fully elsewhere,[17] this amounts to a recovery of the classicist ideal (dominant in Hegel) of an aesthetics-ethics as the harmonious conciliation of the singular (or the singular experience, or the singular historical community) in a whole that may have value only insofar as it is an articulated and open presence. Would this be so far removed from the incontrovertibility of metaphysical foundations that are, for hermeneutics, to be broken down as the root of violence and of the forgetting of Being?

A reorientation of the stance of the ethics of continuity to nihilism is necessary precisely in order to avoid a similar risk that, here too, would entail a betrayal of the specific stimuli behind hermeneutics and, at the same time, its transformation into a general and excessively weak philosophy of culture. In conclusion, let us try once more to delineate the difference it makes to ethics if the nihilistic vocation of hermeneutics is taken up explicitly. One thing is certain: the theoretical legitimacy of our attempt is linked as much to the need to respond positively to the original anti-metaphysical inspiration (which means here that one cannot rest with the Hegelian ideal of conciliation with the totality), as to the related need to appropriate one's own historicity. On this basis, it becomes clear not only that the ideal of continuity is historically situated (for example it is linked to eighteenth- and nineteenth-century classicism and its background), but also that, if the ideal is acknowledged, the continuity in which it is a case of integrating oneself is the continuity of a history whose meaning we must put ourselves at risk to determine. It seems impossible to define the meaning of the history of modernity, or of the epoch of Being to which hermeneutics must respond, otherwise than as nihilism. The hermeneutic ethic of continuity is therefore the call to place single experiences within a network of connections that seem to us to be oriented towards the dissolution of Being, and thereby towards the reduction of the authority of presence. The arguments required – in line with the Habermasian version of hermeneutic ethics as the ethics of communication – in order to identify and defend to others the moral preferability of one choice, or in Rorty's case one system of redescription, over another are not entrusted to a general (transcendental, panoramic) capacity for integration into the continuity of any particular tradition, community or social fabric. It is here and now that ethics expresses itself as an imperative of continuity – with the proviso that it appeals to a specific sense of the here and now, and more particularly to an interpretative hypothesis about the meaning (of the history) of Being, which it regards as oriented towards a progressive weakening in the authority of presence.[18]

Might it not be easier to argue against the fundamentalisms and communitarianisms reappearing all across the late-modern world from the point of view of nihilism rather than from that of Habermas, Rorty or even Gadamer? It is not by chance that this issue should have presented itself here, almost spontaneously. For it may be that the epoch of the end of metaphysics to which the ethics of hermeneutics means to cor-respond is distinguished not only by the dissolution of the principle of reality into the Babel of interpretations and the phantasmagoria of the technological world, but also and indelibly by the dissolution of fundamental-isms of every kind; it is not hard to see them as neurotic defences of identity and belonging in reaction to the indefinite widening of horizons entailed by the culmination of the epoch of the world

picture. Without a clear appropriation of its own nihilistic vocation, hermeneutic ethics can only respond to this situation by
seeking to contain it, as if it were essentially a matter of defending
a kernel of values that are under threat and inexorably destined
to be swept away. This, on close inspection, is the tenor, the
Stimmung, of hermeneutic humanism's attitude towards the
techno-scientific society. However, Heidegger has taught us that
modern technology is the direct consequence of Platonic metaphysics. This does not mean, as some believe, that responsibility
for the degeneration in our humanity caused by science and
technology must be traced back to Plato. Standing within the
course of the history of metaphysics, modern techno-science, with
all that it implies for the life of the individual and of society,
nonetheless displays a certain logic, a guiding thread to which
one can appeal in order to tell what 'goes' and what 'does not
go'. Instead of reacting to the dissolution of the principle of
reality by attempting to recuperate a sense of identity and belonging that are at once reassuring and punitive, it is a matter of
grasping nihilism as a *chance* [in English in the original] of
emancipation.

To reveal the world as a conflict of interpretations also means,
however, to recognize ourselves as heirs to a tradition of the
weakening of the strong structures of Being in every field of
experience – heirs, and therefore relations, daughters, brothers
and friends of those to whose calls we must now cor-respond.
Thinking that no longer understands itself as the recognition and
acceptance of an objective authoritarian foundation will develop
a new sense of responsibility as ready and able, literally, to
respond to others whom, insofar as it is not founded on the
eternal structure of Being, it knows to be its 'provenance'. *Amica
veritas, sed magis amicus Plato*, perhaps. Is it chance that some
philosophers (beyond suspicion of spiritualism) speak today about
a principle of charity?[19] But will this not be simply to uncover
another eternal 'metaphysical' value to replace that of truth?
More probably, we shall rediscover no more than a word within
the same nihilistic tradition, a word that has been spoken author-
itatively and that is perhaps the most decisive among those which
philosophy should reappropriate, through loyalty to its own
provenance. This is not an obscure and numinous illusion, a

rhetorical ornament of discourse. The next step in the exploration of the meaning of hermeneutics for philosophy must be to come to terms with the religious tradition, beginning with that of Western Europe.

4

Religion

As the nihilisitic implications of its own premisses are developed, hermeneutics encounters charity and so rediscovers its own links with the Western religious tradition. This is no accident. It is simply another, probably more radical, way of experiencing its own concrete historicity, its belonging to modernity – or perhaps a way that this may be radicalized retrospectively along the lines followed earlier by the reflection on science and ethics.

Hermeneutics belongs to modernity inasmuch as the grounds of its 'truth' (there are no facts, only interpretations) may only be set forth on the basis of the fulfilment within nihilism of the principle of reality which it regards as characteristic of modernity. But modernity is the child of the Western religious tradition, above all as the secularization of this tradition. It seems that hermeneutics has not only been a consequence of modern secularization (as a philosophy born out of the dissolution of the metaphysics of objectivity), but was also an important contributory factor; for the breakdown of catholic unity in Europe was heavily influenced by the new way of reading the Bible based on the Lutheran principle of 'scripture alone', but also and perhaps above all by the rationalist exegeses set in train by Spinoza. When Dilthey, in his essay on 'The Origins of Hermeneutics', speaks (in connection with Baur) of the 'liberation of exegesis from dogma',[1] he is referring to what is for him a fundamental element in the rise of modern hermeneutics. After Dilthey, and beyond him, it becomes

clear that in order to become a general theory of interpretation
(and of existence as interpretation) hermeneutics must cease to be
identified with a series of rules for the comprehension of a special
category of texts, in the face of which it is never more than a pure
technique, subordinate and instrumental, whose significance
depends entirely on the weight attributed to the text itself. From
the point of view of hermeneutics taken exclusively as an instru-
ment of biblical exegesis, the truth of existence is primarily the
revealed history of creation–sin–redemption, and only because of
this is it important to understand, via interpretation, the word of
God entrusted to us in the scriptures. This framework seems to
preclude the birth of a nihilistic thesis like that, apparently
characteristic of hermeneutics in the philosophical sense, according to which there are no facts, only interpretations.

The link between hermeneutics and the emancipation from
dogma (or, if one prefers, the step towards a consideration of the
sacred text as a text amongst others) seems in any case fairly
obvious if one thinks of the importance for the modern reading of
the Bible of the rationalistic attitude epitomized by the *Tractatus
theologico-politicus* of Spinoza. And moreover, it is clearly prefig-
ured by more ancient literary hermeneutics (I am thinking here of
the allegorical interpretation of deeds of the Homeric heroes,
reflected in Greek philosophy as the need to save the divine from
the irrationality of myth[2]). In short, modern hermeneutics is
developed against a strong rationalistic background, albeit not
always as extreme and explicit as that of Spinoza, and it therefore
seems quite natural to share Dilthey's view of it as an aspect of
the general movement of secularization characteristic of modernity. This makes it hard to explain the 'rediscovery' of the Christian
religious tradition that we seemed to detect in the conclusion of
the discourse on hermeneutic ethics and on the 'principle of
charity'.

Dilthey's schema places hermeneutics in a context that, in
Gadamer's words, can only be defined as 'historiographical
enlightenment'.[3] It is precisely the difficulties inherent in this
perspective – which is still deeply marked by the reference to the
natural sciences as an unquestioned methodological model, in
spite of all their differences – that explain the essential incompleteness of Dilthey's theory and many of his writings on the matter.

Heidegger's subsequent ontological radicalization of the relation between temporality and the historicity of existence allowed hermeneutics to free itself from the burden of this methodological model. From the point of view made possible by Heidegger's existential analytic, significantly at the basis also of Gadamer's hermeneutics, the history of modernity is instead the history of the imposition of a scientific conception of truth, and thus the history of the progressive affirmation of the enlightenment; but it also the history of a process via which our awareness of the essentially interpretative character of every consciousness of truth has been lost. The development of hermeneutics has followed, for a certain time and in certain respects, the affirmation of the Enlightenment: in Schleiermacher (who, at least in Gadamer's view, conceived of interpretation as an identification with the object to be understood, and so still in terms of objective fidelity); and in Dilthey (who sought to determine a method able to guarantee a still scientific kind of validity). Yet the unresolved contradictions and wholesale inadequacies of theories such as these, and above all the continued existence of hermeneutic positions that are more faithful to an interpretative experience irreducible to objective mirroring (Gadamer, as is well known, finds the bases of the theory of hermeneutic truth in the Hegelian idea of the experience of consciousness), both support a view of hermeneutics not as part of the Enlightenment project, but rather as a kind of minor trend that survives into modern culture, drawing its vigour from Heidegger and, before that, from pheno-menology and the meditations of Count Yorck.

This is not the occasion to reconstruct the whole of this process, which is described by Gadamer in the long historical section (the second) of *Truth and Method*. It need be recalled only because, once again as in the case of the themes addressed in preceding chapters, it is in Gadamer that we can find the bases of a possible standard hermeneutic theory on the problem of religion – one that is built along lines that are broadly common to, yet rarely thematically stated by Pareyson and Ricoeur, in addition to Gadamer himself (though not Rorty). On the basis of this (let me repeat, often implicit) standard theory, hermeneutics presents itself as a thinking that is well disposed towards religion, in that its critique of the idea of truth as verifiable conformity between proposition and thing undermines the rationalist, empiricist, positivist and even idealist and Marxist negations of the possibility of religious experience. It may not offer any positive argument to recommend a religious vision of life, in that it contains nothing resembling the *preambula fidei* of the scholastic tradition, but it certainly dissolves the bases of the principal arguments that philosophy has offered in favour of atheism.

All this seems somewhat vague and general. In the case of the problem of religion, as in that of the relation with modern science with which we began, contemporary hermeneutics seems to be only, or above all, a theory that frees reason from its slavery to the scientistic ideal of objectivity, only to pave the way to a philosophy of culture whose limits (and meaning) cannot ultimately be determined. Having dissolved the metaphysical ideal of truth as conformity, primarily thanks to Heidegger, hermeneutics lends fresh plausibility to religion and even myth, quite independently of any Hegelian-style historicist justification (that would treat them as necessary stages of the development of reason, now overcome but with their essential content preserved). From this perspective, one might well see a further sign of the pervasiveness of the hermeneutic *koiné* in the widespread use in recent philosophically minded journalism (primarily in Italy, but not exclusively so[4]) of terms and ideas belonging to the mythological and religious tradition of the West that have been extracted from their original context without any theoretical justification whatsoever. It is probably a matter of a cultural tendency arising from the legacy of thinkers such as Franz Rosenzweig or Walter Benjamin who are deeply rooted in the Hebraic tradition, without entirely lacking (at least in the case of the former) a clear impulse to systematicity. This is sometimes legitimated by an implicit assumption of the necessity for philosophy to enter into dialogue with poetry, which might then serve as an intermediary between religious myth and rational thought in a fashion well known to the history of Western culture and perhaps (see the following chapter) more significant than one might believe, even for a nihilistic radicalization of hermeneutics. Another reason for the diffusion of mythologico-poetico-religious terminology in current philosophical prose may be found in the significance attached to a model or repertory of figures, like that developed by psychoanalysis. In its Jungian form, it speaks explicitly of polytheism[5] – and it is precisely of polytheism that those theories which defend the value of the human sciences often speak, moreover in a sense very close to hermeneutics understood as philosophy of culture.[6] Finally, it seems likely that the hermeneutic critique of the objectivist ideal of truth leads to the recognition of the essentially metaphorical character of every language, thereby justifying the rejection of any proposal to reduce metaphorical expressions (myth, poetry etc.) to 'proper' discourse characterized by the philosophical *logos* (a position that one meets explicitly in 'hermeneutic' authors like Paul Ricoeur and Jacques Derrida).

But all this, with varying degrees of complexity and richness of 'associations', ultimately amounts (and here we do not shirk moving to the 'proper') to treating hermeneutics as a 'negative' philosophy, in a sense perhaps distantly related to the Schellingian, that is, to a thinking that liberates the 'positive' aspect of mythological, religious and poetic discourses from the obstacles of the rationalistic ideal of truth as objectivity.

Yet, once again, is this liberation in its turn the (metaphysical) recognition that reality is plural, that there are many ways, irreducible to one another, of saying the true, without there being any supreme case by which they are legitimated and placed in a hierarchy? Two expressions archetypical of the philosophical and religious tradition of the West echo forth: the *to on léghetai pollachôs* (Being is said in many ways) of Aristotle, and the 'multifariam multisque modis olim loquens Deus patribus in prophetis' of St Paul[7] – displaced (or, to be precise, metaphorized) outside of their context, which in the first case is provided by the Aristotelian idea of substance, and in the second by a key event (the incarnation of the son of God) conferring meaning on the many preceding and succeeding events. In some way, it is between these two extremes that the problem unfolds not only of the relation of hermeneutics to the religious tradition, but also of its philosophical meaning as a whole. But is a recovery of the Aristotelian conception of the plurivocity of Being, as seems to be underway in today's hermeneutic *koiné*, actually possible without the keel of substance – thus without a hierarchy, without a 'first by analogy' (a 'proper' meaning), without a supreme metaphysical case? The meaning of nihilistic ontology that we are trying here to discern in hermeneutics is rather the outcome of a 'contamination' of Aristotelian pluralism by Pauline 'historicism'. For Aristotelian ontological pluralism, even denuded of its reference to substance, remains a objectivistic-metaphysical thesis (the Being is said in many ways because, and only because, it *is* in many ways – irreducible to be sure, yet nonetheless articulated as one in the sole descriptive proposition that 'reflects' them in their plurality), that is, as we have argued above, ultimately untenable from a hermeneutic perspective. To avoid the contradiction, it would seem necessary to place the same affirmation of the plurivocity of Being – or, in our terms, of the interpretative character of every experience of truth – in the framework of a history of Being (interpreted) as a history of the weakening of its strong structures. In this way, the plurality of meanings of Being are given in a framework akin to that marked out by St Paul.

Is it just a matter of analogy, of a metaphorical slippage again, justified on the basis of the emancipation of metaphor from the slavery of the proper that hermeneutics in fact promotes? From such a perspective, the meeting between hermeneutic ethics and the 'principle of charity' would be no more than a feature of this slippage; merely another appeal by philosophical prose to religious-poetic images made possible by the emancipation of thought from the ideal of objectivity. But here one is faced with yet another configuration of the contradictory character of hermeneutics taken in the broad and vague sense of the *koiné*. For in theorizing its own constitutive historicity, can hermeneutics state that it thinks this historicity on the basis of a model that it recognizes as belonging to its own history and that it nonetheless freely adopts as an available conceptual tool that may be used 'without consequences' and without any particular responsibility? Can one speak, in short, of angels, the divine trinity, incarnation and redemption, without posing the problem of what relation we are to assume to the 'dogmatic' sense that these terms have had in the tradition that has transmitted them to us?

The issue here is this. Contrary to the Diltheyan idea (common amongst Enlightenment conceptions of modernity) that the development of hermeneutics as 'general philosophy' followed its emancipation from the dogmatism in which it was bound as a technique in the service of biblical exegesis, it is a matter of recognizing that it can rediscover its own authentic meaning as nihilistic ontology only if it recovers its substantial link, at source, with the Judaeo-Christian tradition as the constitutive tradition of the West. In other words: modern hermeneutic philosophy is born in Europe not only because here there is a religion of the book that focuses attention on the phenomenon of interpretation, but also because this religion has at its base the idea of the incarnation of God, which it conceives as *kenosis*, as abasement and, in our translation, as weakening.

The emphasis laid – not accidentally – on the incarnation as *kenosis* also resolves the problem that arises when Aristotelian plurivocity, which follows necessarily from the reference to a basis in substance (and which one does not elude by grounding the plurivocity, no less metaphysically, in the *structural* multiplicity of Being), is replaced by the 'prophetic' plurivocity of St Paul. Here too, it seems, there remains a founding moment that, as in the Hegelian idea of the *Aufhebung* (the dialectical overcoming), at once conserves and suppresses the truth of the prophecies. From a Hegelian perspective like this, Jesus Christ did not prove the prophets wrong; he revealed their true sense while at the same time exposing their limits, rendering them inessential and obsolete: their truth was such only because it was realized in his life and revealed in his teaching. Once again, God and Jesus Christ are thought here in the light of an idea of truth as the objective articulation of evidence that, as it becomes definitive, renders interpretation superfluous. Note that in the history of the church this schema operates, more or less covertly, in an essentially disciplinary manner (I am thinking primarily, but not exclusively, of the Catholic church): the revelation somehow concluded with the coming of Christ, the scriptural canon was fulfilled, and the interpretation of the sacred texts became ultimately the concern only of the Pope and the cardinals. But alongside this dogmatic-disciplinarian view of the revelation, which seems in the end to be discredited by its profound indebtedness to objectivistic metaphysics, the history of Christianity is traversed by another wholly different thread that one might well call Joachimist: for it was Joachim of the Flowers who spoke of a third age in the histories of humanity and of salvation, namely, the reign of the spirit (following after that of the Father in the Old Testament, and that of the Son), in which the 'spiritual' sense of the scriptures is increasingly in evidence, with charity taking the place of discipline. Rather than following Joachim, however,[8] it is a matter here of taking *kenosis* seriously. Against this very broadly Joachimist tradition, one can set the pages where Schleiermacher dreams of a religion in which everyone can be the author of their own Bible;[9] or those of Novalis, in which a re-evaluation of the 'aesthetic' aspects of religiosity (the images, the Madonna, the rituals) runs alongside the same dream of a Christianity that is no longer dogmatic or disciplinarian.[10] Only the alliance between the Enlightenment rigour of anti-religious rationalism and the disciplinary rigour of the churches has in general confined these perspectives to the margins of the history of modern thought, as though they were reducible to an attempt to identify religion with a generic religious attitude, at once 'natural', aesthetic and sentimental – against which should be set the 'true' essence of religion as the experience of an encounter with a God that is 'wholly other' and that as such threatens neither the integral fabric of the Enlightenment dream of rationalism nor the disciplinary radicalism, closed to any kind of secularization, imposed by the dogmatisms of the churches.

To recognize the place of hermeneutics within the religious tradition of the West (not only insofar as this tradition, founded as it is on scriptural revelation, encourages thinking to recognize the centrality of interpretation; nor only because, in liberating thinking from the myth of objectivity, hermeneutics allows the many religious myths of humanity to be heard; but in substantial terms of the links between nihilistic ontology and the *kenosis* of God) is also to encounter problems like these concerning the reinterpretation of the meaning of Christianity within our own culture. If one discovers that hermeneutics is closely related to dogmatic Christianity, neither the meaning of hermeneutics nor that of dogmatics will be left intact.

As regards the latter, to which we can refer here only briefly since it is not our principal theme, the relation with hermeneutics produces a critical rethinking of its disciplinary character: the nihilistic 'drift' that hermeneutics reads in the 'myth' of incarnation and crucifixion does not cease with the conclusion of Jesus's time on earth, but continues with the descent of the Holy Spirit and with the interpretation of this revelation by the community of believers. According to the line that, with no pretence to philological accuracy, I propose to call here Joachimist, the meaning of scripture in the age opened by the descent of the Holy Spirit becomes increasingly 'spiritual' and thereby less bound to the rigour of dogmatic definitions and strict disciplinarian observance. It is not difficult to see how this can serve as a basis for a reading of various conflicts that, in the past and perhaps above all of late, have set the community (or communities) of believers against the ecclesiastical hierarchy (above all in the Catholic church), on specific points of ethics and also, broadly speaking, of dogmatics (for example, on the question of women priests, which is not simply a moral issue): for the most part, the ecclesiastical hierarchy defends the 'authentic' meaning of the Christian message against what it regards as secularizing and modish interpretations that are altogether too soft and conciliatory. More or less the same things were said many times against the religious attitude of Schleiermacher and Novalis.

But will the same secularization not be rather a 'drift' inscribed positively in the destiny of *kenosis*? As regards the meaning of dogmatic Christianity, it is to this question that the recognition of a 'substantial' relation with hermeneutics ultimately leads. Moreover, this movement is helped along by René Girard's theories on violence and the sacred[11] – even if he does not himself push them as far as these conclusions (and at bottom it is not clear why not). Girard, we recall here in the briefest of terms, sees the natural religions as founded on a victim-based conception of the sacred: when serious conflicts break out within the community, the way to heal them is to concentrate on a single (sacrificial) scapegoat the violence that would otherwise be unleashed against everyone. Since the scapegoat functions effectively to reduce the violence, it assumes a sacral and divine character. The meaning of the Old and New Testaments, however, is to reveal the falsehood of the sacred as violent and natural. Jesus, most especially, comes to be put to death not because he is the perfect victim, as has always been understood, but because he is the bearer of a message too radically in contrast with the deepest (sacral and victim-based) convictions of all the 'natural' religions. The extraordinary character of his revelation (the sacred is not sacrificial violence, God is

Love) demonstrates, amongst other things, that he could not be only human.

Girard, as I have said, does not seek to extend his thesis into a genuine theory of secularization as the authentic destiny of Christianity (and not as its abandonment and negation). Yet there are good reasons for such an extension. To begin with the history of European modernity, it would be too naive and schematic to conceive of it as an emancipation from the Christian tradition, for in many respects – from capitalist economics (in Max Weber's famous thesis) to the transformation of despotism into democratic constitutional states, to the general 'humanization' of interpersonal relations (yes, precisely that humanitarianism that Nietzsche so despised, and that more recently Foucault has understood as no more than a sophisticated way of affirming a wide-reaching disciplinary structure in society) – one cannot think of it otherwise than as an 'application', albeit not literal, perhaps distorted, of the Christian (and before that Judaic) legacy. Aside from the positions that refute the very idea of modernity as secularization (such as Blumenberg's[12]) – and which seem untenable to us by virtue of the fact that they do not give sufficient consideration to the historical roots of modernity in the ancient and medieval tradition – the objections that in general, above all by believers, are raised against this vision of the secularization as a destiny 'proper' to Christianity concern the possibility of establishing a criterion that permits the distinction of secularization from phenomena that confine themselves to applying the Christian tradition, often in a distorted fashion, yet which are themselves outside or indeed in opposition to it. Yet it is precisely here that one should rediscover the 'principle of charity' which, perhaps not by accident, constitutes the point of convergence between nihilistic hermeneutics and the religious tradition of the West. Secularization has no 'objective' limit: the Augustinian 'ama et fac quod vis' holds even for the interpretation of the scriptures. For dogmatic Christianity (that is, the substance of New Testament revelation), recognition of its relation with nihilistic hermeneutics means the emergence of charity as the single most decisive factor of the evangelical message.

But none of this – the consequences of the 'relation' seen from the side of dogmatics, what becomes of the faith of a believing

Christian who also 'believes' in the radical version of hermeneutics we have put forward – is our principal concern here. For, without aiming at a 'panoramic' vision of any kind (hermeneutics and science, hermeneutics and ethics, hermeneutics and religion, etc.), this is to clarify the significance of the philosophy of interpretation, once liberated from metaphysical misconstrual, for thinking the relation between philosophy and religion. In view of the need not to fall back into metaphysical objectivism, it appeared that this relation could take the form neither of a pure and simple relegitimation of religious myth (on the basis of Aristotle's *to on léghetai pollachôs* separated – but by what right? – from the fundamental reference to substance), or of a recognition of myth and religion as necessary stages in a development of reason towards its own maturity (Hegelian historicism).

In place of these two kinds of relation, we are looking here to determine another, which takes more seriously, as it were, the belonging of hermeneutics to modernity, conceived above all as the secularization of the religious tradition of the West. However, when the idea of secularization is considered in relation to hermeneutics, it has seemed to us far more difficult to arrive at a univocal definition of it than is commonly believed: paradoxically in fact, hermeneutics, whose Enlightenment origins are demythologizing and rationalistic in inspiration, leads in contemporary thinking to the dissolution of the very myth of objectivity (this is the meaning of the radical demythification worked by Nietzsche[13]) and to the 'rehabilitation' of myth and religion. Ultimately, it is this paradox that – if one were to phrase the whole argument of this chapter so far in strictly logical form – draws our attention back to the most intimate of relations between hermeneutics and the Christian tradition: nihilism is too much 'like' *kenosis* for one to see this likeness as simply a coincidence, an association of ideas. We are led to the hypothesis that hermeneutics itself, as a philosophy with certain ontological commitments, is the fruit of secularization as the renewal, pursuit, 'application' and interpretation of the substance of the Christian revelation, and preeminently the dogma of the incarnation of God. In this way, if one's understanding of how and why hermeneutics cannot be a philosophy well disposed towards religion is based solely on the meaning of the Aristotelian *to on léghetai pollachôs*, it is not commensurately clear how or why the relation of hermeneutics with religion does not assume a Hegelian form in which the religious tradition is interpreted and thereby *aufgehoben*, its form suppressed and its content conserved, by the rationality of philosophical discourse in which its definitive truth is put into language. There are at least two reasons why this Hegelian relation of *Aufhebung* does not hold for hermeneutics. First, it still assumes the ideal of objectivity whose eventual coincidence with the subject makes it possible to speak of a definitive attainment of the truth. Second, or simply from a different perspective, could there ever be an *Aufhebung* to match the advance of a 'kenotic' tendency that belongs from the first to the very content of revelation? It seems, in short, that one cannot think the Hegelian overcoming otherwise than in view of growth, elevation (one of the senses of *aufheben*), appropriation: all of which are wholly contrary to the divine *kenosis* spoken of by the Gospels.

In the final analysis, the philosophical appropriation of the truth of religion still takes place in accordance with a law of philosophy, of the reason that reconciles itself to itself. But the *kenosis* that occurs as the incarnation of God and most recently as secularization and the weakening of Being and its strong structures (to the point of the dissolution of the ideal of truth as objectivity) takes place in accordance with a 'law' of religion, at least in the sense that it is not by its own decision that the subject is committed to a process of ruin, for one finds oneself called to such a commitment by the 'thing itself'. The idea underpinning hermeneutics of the belonging of the interpreter to the 'thing' to be interpreted, or more generally to the game of interpretation, mirrors, expresses, repeats and interprets this experience of transcendence. The difficulty of finding the right term for the relation between the hermeneutic experience of belonging to the thing itself and the religious experience of transcendence confirms that it is not easy to quit the traditional metaphysical configurations of the philosophy–religion relation (the 'Aristotelian' relation of ontological pluralism; and the Hegelian relation of *Aufhebung*). And yet Heidegger quite clearly tells us that, in this case too, with regard to the metaphysical tradition one cannot do otherwise than establish a relation of *Verwindung*:[14] of resigned acceptance, of continuation, of (dis)tortion.[15] Which means, here, that we must not be surprised if, in the effort of thinking the relation from the perspective of hermeneutics, we rediscover certain aspects of the two metaphysical configurations to which we have referred. Effectively, thinking of itself as the heir of modernity, hermeneutics also thinks of its own relation with the religious tradition as a historical provenance that has something of the Hegelian dialectical overcoming: in the secularization that hermeneutics itself is, the content of Christian revelation is preserved as it assumes different forms. On the other hand, precisely because it is not governed by the ideal of ultimate self-transparency and full reappropriation, this process is only the liberation of the plurality of the senses of Being, in the sense that we have, for convenience, called Aristotelian.

This is as far as we can go: the liberation of the plurality of myths, and thus the re-legitimation of religion in the wake of hermeneutics, are wholly dependent on a process of secularization set in train by the story of the *kenosis* of God in the incarnation. If the legitimation of this plurality were underpinned solely by the structural multivocity of Being itself, it would in truth become untenable. One cannot do without substance in Aristotle – even the pure and simple affirmation of the irreducible multivocity of Being would always be the object of a 'unitary' metaphysical affirmation. Transposing this into the frame of our own enquiry: when, as often happens, philosophy in general and hermeneutics in particular declare that there are many ways of having an experience of truth (for example that myth is an 'other' way alongside the *logos*), this is stated as *logos*, which is implicitly affirmed as the superior form. A myth or religion that theorizes the possibility of philosophy alongside itself and with equal rights has yet to be born.

Hermeneutics can be what it is – a non-metaphysical philosophy with an essentially interpretative attitude towards truth, and thus a nihilistic ontology – only as heir to the Christian myth of the incarnation of God. Perhaps the only hermeneutic philosopher to have provided the instruments to think this condition through radically was Luigi Pareyson, for whom philosophy was the hermeneutics of religious experience[16] – which he referred to, in no sense pejoratively, as myth. To him, philosophy could not but reflect on the experience of a transcendence given originarily in the form of myth, that is, as the 'symbolic' presence of the divine in the visible. The mythic character of the encounter with the divine does not arise from the roughness of human faculties yet to be educated in rational thought. It arises from the essence of the transcendent itself, which is revealed only in speaking to the whole of man as a natural being, imposing itself in forms that cannot be appropriated, as is the case with myth, poetry and languages charged with images and emotions. But that the transcendent is given in this way and not only by virtue of the immaturity of the human faculties is something that we learn only from the incarnation of God in Jesus Christ. Christ – at least it seems to me that Pareyson's premiss may be developed in this way – is not just a special case of a 'generic' sensible revelation of God: it is He that makes possible, through his incarnation, every symbolic manifestation of the divine. Christ does not undermine the myths and stories of false and lying gods: he makes their signification of the divine possible for the first time. If we accept Pareyson's use of the term in a Schellingian sense to mean, in contrast to allegory, the full presence of the symbolized in its sensible manifestation,[17] we shall be unable to take Christ as opening the way to a recognition of ancient myths as partially and provisionally true, yet rendered obsolete by his coming, for which the term allegory would in fact be more appropriate.

The consequences of these premises, which Pareyson was unable or unwilling to develop fully, are dense and complex. It is not a matter of using the Gospel paradoxically to re-evaluate ancient mythologies, but rather of rethinking more concretely the secularization of Christianity as a liberation of the plurality of myths, not only the ancient myths, but also and above all those of religions with which Christian ecumenicalism deals today: a liberation made possible by the incarnation of Jesus, that is, by the *kenosis* of God. The question of ecumenicalism might be put like this: what can be the relation between Christianity and other religions with which it has come into ever more intense contact in modernity and that, in modernity, it can no longer treat as errors – precisely because the experience of encountering them has left it unable to think of itself as the sole objective and exhaustive metaphysical truth (missions can no longer follow in the footsteps of colonists)? Its importance is not only for theology and the churches: it is a problem that also bears upon hermeneutics as the philosophy of modernity, in the various senses referred to in earlier chapters. Indeed, it may well be that the question of ecumenicalism appears so central only because we see in it simply another configuration of the problem around which our discourse has been moving from the first: that of not reducing hermeneutics to a simple, metaphysical, pluralist philosophy of culture, with a tendency towards relativism and, ultimately, the frivolous. But that one arrives at this other configuration is not without significance for the clarification of the meaning of hermeneutics for philosophy. For the question of ecumenicalism provides a crucial link between the problematic of the universality of philosophical truth and the destiny of the West. The solution that its version of hermeneutics is inclined to give to the question of the universality of the true is ultimately modelled, as we know, on Kant's *Critique of Judgement*. The views of the hermeneutic philosopher are put forward not on the basis of demonstration, but almost as judgements of taste whose universality arises from an always contingent consensus straining towards expansion. Although the model has been appropriated theoretically, it always risks appearing too aesthetic, too disincarnate, if it does not take into consideration the concreteness of historical situations in which judgement is made and put to the consensus of others. If one forces oneself to imagine the concrete conditions in which this game of call and response takes place, what one finds is a framework within which are mixed two kinds of experience: aesthetic and religious. On the one hand, both the fundamental importance, for hermeneutics, of the defence of the truth of art found in a classic text such as *Truth and Method*, and the 'aestheticism' of Rorty's theory of redescriptions show that the plurality of the *Weltanschauungen*, of those all-embracing theories that are at once indispensable to both individuals and groups and irreducible to the demonstrative universality of scientific propositions, can only be thought by 'lay' philosophy under the category of art and aesthetics. On the other hand, however, a different and more powerful type of global theory continues to stand in opposition to that modelled on the plurality of the artistic 'openings', namely, the world of religious doctrines and the churches. If in discovering the non-univocal meaning of secularization hermeneutics becomes aware of its own place within the history of salvation narrated in the Bible, it will not be able to rest with a vision of secularization as a linear and progressive departure from the Christian tradition, where the present *Weltanschauung* is seen to assume the form of aesthetics, in contrast to an apparently earlier religious configuration that is to be 'overcome'. One does not escape this presentation of the problem by satisfying oneself that art and religion, and ultimately philosophy, are simply different ways of getting at the truth that do not conflict with one another; for in this way one would simply return to the purely metaphysical panoramic-objectivistic sense of the Aristotelian *to on léghetai pollachôs*. Therefore it seems as though hermeneutics cannot avoid confronting the problem of aesthetics – not abstractly, as a particular experience to describe alongside other experiences in its conditions of possibility, but in the concrete and constitutive relation with religion in which art has come to find itself in the course of the process of secularization that characterizes modernity.

5

Art

❧

As a point of departure, let us take an experience that is probably common to most of us as citizens of the advanced industrial world whose duties as consumers include that of cultural tourism. Many will undoubtedly have found themselves walking into a church one Sunday morning to see the frescos that decorate the walls, to study the architecture, and to take a closer look at the statues and the bas-reliefs. But it is Sunday, there is a mass in progress, and the faithful in their pews are devoutly intent on prayer or attentive to the homily. The cultural tourist, although (as is more and more often the case) unchecked by the sign reading 'No entry for tourists during services', moves with a certain embarrassment and is conscious of being a disturbance, and out of place. Those in prayer regard tourists with mixed feelings, for on the one hand they should welcome them with a charitable attitude, respectful of their interests and the intentions that have brought them to their church. Yet on the other hand they sense in tourists a foreignness in conflict with what, at least at that moment, seems to them to be the proper meaning of the place. An analogous situation, symmetrically reversed, would occur if a believer in the Madonna and Saints were to enter one of the many museums of art frequented for the purposes of 'aesthetic' contemplation, and kneel down before an altarpiece. This second situation is far less common, indeed it has probably never happened; although this too should give us pause for thought. In any case, while tourists are denied entrance to churches only during the hours of mass, no museum has ever reserved a portion of its opening hours for believers who wished to pray before paintings of religious subjects.

Experiences such as these appear neither particularly relevant nor, above all, problematic from the perspective prevailing in modern aesthetics, which has become used to resolving the question along the lines of the sign reading 'Tourists are not permitted to visit while religious services are in progress'. There is a time for the religious use of sacred buildings and there is a time for their aesthetic enjoyment. It is pointless trying to say who is right between the faithful going to Sant'Ivo della Sapienza solely (or principally) to pray, having only a 'distracted perception' for the architectural wonder of the place (like that which Walter Benjamin believed was most natural and most suitable for architecture and which at bottom he considered most authentic[1]), or the visitors interested in enjoying the masterpiece by Borromini; for the two types of interest correspond to two dimensions of human experience that we (moderns) have learnt to distinguish by recognizing their specific rights. In church one prays, in the museum one aesthetically enjoys works of art. And even when the two experiences take place in the same space, one can easily resolve the conflict by a careful division of 'times' – although it still remains a little unclear why it is the churches that contrive this division of times and not rather the museums. Interpreted radically, this fact could only signify an intrusion of the problematic of secularization into the apparent order of the 'modern' distinction between the different types of experience: inasmuch as the distinction between the various dimensions of experience acknowledges the rights proper to each, and yet cannot avoid affirming a certain 'superiority' of that dimension which theorizes and establishes those rights. In this way, pushing the argument just a little further, it is clearly the dimension of the museum that is in control, as in the final analysis even the faithful at prayer in Sant'Ivo alla Sapienza are assigned their place as 'museum-pieces' to be respected alongside the works of art that they continue to 'use' for an end not their 'own', that is, not purely aesthetic and thus foreign to the dimension to which they specifically belong.

As far as art is concerned, hermeneutics is of course characterized precisely by the challenge it poses to the ideology of the museum via its critique of 'aesthetic consciousness' as that attitude which, as a complement to modern scientism, assigns to art a dimension of experience wholly separate from that wherein one deals with truth. It was in defence of the capacity of art to convey truth that Gadamer, as we have noted several times already, paved the way for a recognition of the interpretative character of all human experience. But how is all this reflected in our understanding of what, for convenience, we shall call the 'Sant'Ivo experience'? It seems, once again, that what a hermeneutics clearly aware of its own nihilistic vocation must do is to renew and to radicalize the standard hermeneutic positions that, even on the problem of art, permeate the *koiné* that the philosophy of interpretation has now become. The radicalization, as should be clear by now, consists in placing the classical theses of hermeneutics, primarily those of Gadamer, within a framework of the history of nihilism as the history of modernity and thereby of secularization.

In its standard form, hermeneutics has led aesthetics to renew its interest in art as an experience of truth, in contrast to an essentially Kantian, and above all neo-Kantian, tradition that has taken root in modernity for which aesthetics is a theory of the specificity of the experience of art privileging what Gadamer, in *Truth and Method*, has called 'aesthetic differentiation'. According to a programme that is still in fact very much alive in recent thinking (inspiring, for example, the Wittgensteinian idea of linguistic therapy via the careful distinction of the specific rules of different linguistic games) progress in philosophy and in rationality in general is achieved by throwing the spotlight on various dimensions of experience and clarifying their specificity, which is then taken as a normative basis for judgement and choice. Clearly, a philosophical attitude of this kind corresponds very closely to modernization as characterized by Max Weber and as, it seems, it has actually unfolded in the last hundred years or so. In this way, we are faced with a situation against which Heidegger, along with most of the early twentieth-century avant-garde, rebelled when he called for thinking to return to the recollection of Being. In spite of the enduring prominence of 'purist' poetics (pure poetry, art for art's sake etc.), even the artistic avant-garde must on the whole be numbered amongst the movements of rebellion against the trend towards specialization and the separation of distinct spheres of existence by virtue of which art too became isolated in a domain entirely separate from those of truth, moral values and concrete social existence.²

All the same, the impression that the hermeneutic rediscovery of the truth of art did not press its conclusions beyond a fairly general level is not without justification. To be sure, the way that we approach the work of art is still decisively influenced by what Gadamer tells us about aesthetic experience as true experience that is transformative of its subject and that cannot be adequately described by theories which continue to rely on Kantian disinterestedness conceived in terms increasingly remote from any ontological point of reference.³ That said, however, if the 'truth' that art contains is to be anything more than a generic form of wisdom about life and human destiny (and this is what one reads in even the least banal of 'prose versions' of poetry), we will have to take up tougher and more explicit positions regarding the relation between truth as discovered in the work of art and truth as sought in philosophy and debate. The clearest example of what I have in mind here is the meditation on the concrete development of the arts found in the second, historical, part of Hegel's *Aesthetics*. It is an example that is not far removed from Gadamer either, who thinks the truth of art precisely on the basis of the Hegelian notion of *Erfahrung*, in which he hears above all the idea of *fahren*, the journey as an experience that transforms and that for this very reason is a bearer of truth. That Gadamer nonetheless does not press much further in the direction we are thinking of here rests once again on the fact that – probably for the best of reasons, alert to the risk of a lapse into some form of strict historicism – he does not situate the recuperation of the truth of art within what Heidegger would call the history of Being.⁴

If it is true that the source of a certain impression of incompleteness that one feels with regard to hermeneutic aesthetics lies, as I believe, in its failure to take on board the whole concrete historicity of the experience of truth given in art, the reason for the significance of the 'Sant'Ivo experience' for our discourse becomes clear. To the questions that it raises one can only respond with a general affirmation of the significance of the truth of aesthetic experience, understood as another possible form of the givenness of truth that can stand quietly alongside that of religious experience. It is not a case of wanting to see conflicts at all costs, nor, as might easily be objected, of having in mind an overly systematic conception of truth intolerant of any pluralism. The point is that the 'Sant'Ivo experience' itself provides a more concrete and precise expression of the initially vague sensation that something was missing from the hermeneutic defence of the truth of art. The premisses developed in the preceding chapters have now led us to think that this something that is missing from hermeneutic aesthetics in its current form (what we call the standard hermeneutic theory) might be found by reflecting on the relation, probably conflictual, between art and religion or, in other terms, on the destiny of art in relation to the process of modern secularization.

It is a theme that seems to have been seldom treated in recent aesthetics, but which has notable precedents and deep and thoroughly respectable theoretical roots. Very probably, when the three founding fathers of German idealism, Hegel, Hölderlin and Schelling, conceived the project which has been handed down to us in the fragment known as the 'Oldest System-Programme of German Idealism',[5] it was less in a spirit of polemic with Kant – and that is, with the very bases of modern aesthetics – than in a spirit of continuation and fulfilment. Here art, and more specifically poetry, is assigned the task of preparing the realization of that realm of liberty which the Parisian revolutionaries had sought in vain to establish (the text dates from a time, namely the period of their friendship at the seminary in Tübingen, when the three friends had already lost faith in the French revolution). The renewal sought here is somewhat akin to that conceived by Schiller in the *Letters on the Aesthetic Education of Man* (1795). Schelling, Hölderlin and Hegel think that the realm of liberty, in which there 'awaits ... the *equal* cultivation of *all* powers, of the individual as well as of all individuals' [my italics], could be realized on the basis of a 'religion of the senses' that is needed not only by the masses, but by the philosopher too. It would be characterized by 'monotheism of reason and of the heart, polytheism of the imagination and art', and would take the form of a 'new mythology' that must, however, 'be at the service of ideas, it must become a mythology of *reason*' [my italics]. It is clear from many aspects of the short essay, not least the opening lines, that the authors see themselves as following on from Kant, from that Kant for whom beauty stood as a symbol of morality. It is worth remembering this spirit of fidelity to Kant in order fully to appreciate that the positions advanced in the 'System-Programme' are by no means foreign to the principal current in modern aesthetics. Only in the course of the nineteenth century, with the rise of positivistic scientism and also, to a considerable extent, neo-Kantianism, did the disinterestedness that Kant attributes to aesthetic experience become a complete disengagement of art in the face of truth. The 'System-Programme' testifies to the fact that Kantianism, even that of the *Critique of Judgement*, could be interpreted in a sense that accentuates the link between art and religion. The religion of the senses the authors envision is perhaps the most striking ideal configuration of an art conceived explicitly as secularized religion. Where the term secularization tells us that while, on the one hand, we are no longer dealing with religion in its original form (another passage in the essay alludes explicitly to the necessity of 'overturning superstition, persecuting the cleric who has for a long time given credit to reason'), on the other hand, the poetic mythology that must replace it is in its own way heir to both the task and the subject matter that once belonged to religion.

The positions on art, religion and new mythology expressed in the 'System-Programme' appeared for the most part to subsequent philosophical aesthetics as too closely bound to German idealism, and to its Romantic phase in particular, for them to be recoverable. Nineteenth- and twentieth-century philosophy of art came to be dominated by the idea that 'progress' in both theoretical aesthetics and the arts themselves be identified with the specialization of the aesthetic experience, its constitution *juxta propria principia* in opposition to every unwarranted conjunction with other activities and other spheres of interest and value (Croce, in spite of all his historicism, takes up a position of the kind with his 'dialectic of the distinct'). Yet even for the aesthetics that follow this trajectory, the relation of art to religion remains 'constitutive', at least in the sense that it is primarily, indeed exclusively, with religion that art has had to avoid being confused in order to affirm its own specificity and exercise its own function in the history of

Western culture. This is perfectly exemplified in Lukács's *Aesthetics*; for he too, like Croce, is historicist and yet steeped in the spirit of neo-Kantianism. According to Lukács, the aesthetic dimension of experience is constituted and theoretically clarified in modernity precisely via a process of emancipation from a dependence that, in late antiquity and the medieval period, always bound the arts (above all the figurative arts, which are not, however, those most socially determinant in which 'the great spiritual turning points occur'[6]) to theology and the church. The superiority of art 'emancipated' from religion over that which carries out the ecclesiastical directive to serve as a Bible for the poor is not only founded, for Lukács, on the achievement of its own specific 'natural' function – although it is very difficult to distinguish between the various motifs among which this is undoubtedly influential. Lukács generally believes that among the different ways in which objectivity is mirrored in pursuit of the general human aim of 'conserving, maintaining and enriching the life' of the species,[7] art and science accomplish a dialectical overcoming of the empirical individuality of the singular person, so facilitating a more 'adequate' (because social) management of the instruments that serve to further this conservation of the life of the species. The inferiority of religion lies in its tendency to conserve individuality as such, which is thereby rendered incapable of mediation with the world and contrasts itself to divine transcendence towards which it can only stand in a relation of submission and irrational faith.[8] I mention Lukács here only because he provides an example of how it is not only abstract and theoretical considerations of modern art that must face the question of secularization as a central question, but also concrete-historical ones too. One might ask, then, to what extent Lukács ends up rediscovering a kind of limit to secularization in that new church that is the communist party: the emancipation of art from individualism (fideism, irrationalism) in which religion remains closed must not, for him, issue in the poetics of the avant-garde, marked by the same sin of individualism and irrationalism, but in an art that is still able to transcend the sphere of individuality and take on an explicit social meaning. Is not Lukács too thinking here of a form of 'rational mythology' capable of taking the role played in medieval art by Christian mythology, which conferred upon the content of art the 'naturalness and the clarity of the immediate phenomenon'[9] (without which it is probably difficult even to conceive of the possibility of an aesthetic experience)?

If indeed, as one could reasonably argue, at the end of his emancipation of aesthetics from its dependence on religion Lukács ultimately rediscovers the church in the form of the party, class etc., the itinerary of his thinking could be taken as an example of a failed process of emancipation; failed precisely insofar as, not recognizing the ambiguity of the very idea of secularization, he ends by believing that the bond with religion has been left definitively behind, whereas it continues to operate all the more powerfully the less one wishes to recognize it.[10]

The ambiguity – and also the fecundity, once it has been thematized – of the bond that subsists between religion and art understood as a moment of the process of modern secularization sounds out, more clearly still than in Lukács, in the essay by Walter Benjamin to which we have already referred, on 'The Work of Art in the Age of Mechanical Reproduction'. It is true that the 'enemy' to be defeated in this case is once again characterized with a religious name, the 'cult value' attributed to the work and to its *hic et nunc*, as though the work of art were a fetish endowed with magic powers (hence the importance of the authenticity of the work and thereby its market value). But the 'expository value' that can serve as an eventual liberation from the advent of the means of the technical reproduction of the work – above all in the arts that are by nature reproducible, such as the cinema – refers back to an aesthetic experience that is no longer specialized, museum-bound and fetishistic, but which may be thought in connection with the 'distracted perception' that the citizens of the city of art reserve for their monuments, largely on the model of the rational mythology that was the ideal of the 'System-Programme'.

The difficulty experienced by Lukács, and probably Benjamin too and perhaps in general by all 'modern' aesthetics that finds the limits of the Kantian and neo-Kantian doctrine of aesthetic disinterestedness too confining, consists, from the perspective that we are trying to clarify here, in the fact that one cannot think secularization in all its significance. The development of art as a specific phenomenon (and of aesthetics as theory) seems bound to the emancipation of art from religion; but when one tries to grasp the meaning of aesthetic experience in its specificity, one is referred back once again to a sphere that resists definition otherwise than in terms of the experience of religion and of myth. It is only natural that this should come to be understood on the strength of the critique levelled by hermeneutics against aesthetic conscious- ness and the differentiation of art. In other words, the critique that seems in Gadamer to have the status above all of a theoretical premiss oriented towards the recuperation of the truth of art, and consequently of the full range of experiences treated by the human sciences, must arrive at a more explicit recognition of its own links with the intentions, or at least the problems, found within the 'System-Programme' of Schelling and his friends. But just as Lukács's idea of secularization is unilateral (as, in a slightly different sense, is Benjamin's), equally unilateral would be a theory like that obscurely adumbrated in the 'System-Programme', which sought to derive from the idea that art has its roots in religion the programme of a pure and simple return to such roots.

What, then, are we to make of things? To be sure, once one has grasped the full significance of the Gadamerian critique of aes- thetic consciousness (that, as I have tried to show elsewhere, finds a point of correspondence in the intolerance of the poetics of the historical avant-garde towards the aesthetic differentiation pre- vailing in nineteenth- and twentieth-century philosophy[11]), one loses all interest in 'systematic' aesthetic theories that strive frantically to define the specific character of art and to derive from it criteria of evaluation, or at least the bases for a re-ordering of experience in the light of a conception of philosophy understood, via Kant, as a reflection on the conditions of possibility. Aesthet- ics, at least from this point of view, can no longer be a reflection on the pure and simple transcendental conditions of possibility of the experience of art and of the beautiful, but must allow itself to listen to the truth that is 'opened' in the work of art. But how will this listening be realized? I have already suggested that it cannot easily be identified with a generic effort to draw philosophical and existential 'truths' from poetry. Aside from being unproductive, this 'method' would also be hard to defend theoretically, if the experience of truth given in art is to be understood, in Gadamer's sense, as a process of transformation in which the reader of the work is implicated (together with the work itself, remember, whose Being is in reality increased by the interpretations it receives). In short, the truth cannot be thought by hermeneutics on the model of the statement. If anything, even that experience of truth which occurs on the basis of a statement (I come to know something, I discover a scientific law etc.) is such only insofar as it transforms whoever is implicated in it. Thus, to rediscover the truth of art cannot even remotely mean to 'prosify' poetry, to derive statements from pictorial works, and so on. Less banal are those positions that insist on the truth of the work as, in Heidegger's words, an 'opening of a world' – an expression that can however be understood in senses that hold for most contemporary aesthetics, from Ernst Bloch to Mikel Dufrenne, to Diltheyan historicism, to Lukács himself. A line of demarcation can be established between all these different positions, which do not all refer explicitly to Heidegger, on the basis of the temporal dimension that is sometimes privileged. Ernst Bloch undoubtedly privileges the future,[12] such that the opening of a world produced by the work is ultimately prophetic in character (but thereby linked to a red emancipatory thread which is somehow already present in history). Dufrenne, who speaks of the work as a 'quasi-subject',[13] a felicitous expression that is also helpful for understanding the 'plausibility' of Heidegger's own position (which otherwise might seem too emphatically and exclusively modelled on the 'epochal' works: the Bible, Dante, Hölderlin and so on) seems to privilege the dimension of the present: at least in the sense that the encounter with the work is an encounter with another vision of the world (but also, in Dufrenne, with another 'aspect' of the ontologically real world that is irreducible to a subjective vision) that modifies our own, and not with a 'thing' introduced peacefully into the world as it stands. Positions like those of Lukács, Dilthey[14] and Gadamer lean towards reading the work of art primarily as a historical document. As for Heidegger, who radically advanced the thesis of the work of art as a setting into work of truth, he seems, in spite of all appearances, to be close to this last position – with the proviso that, for him, the capacity proper to art and poetry of revealing the truth of various historical worlds depends on the inaugural force that the poetic word possesses with respect to these worlds, for which reason it is right to read Heidegger's aesthetics as a 'prophetic' theory of art.

In what sense, and this is the final point that I shall enter into here, can the recognition of art as a phenomenon of secularization, and thus the recognition also of the ambiguous links that connect it with, and separate it from, religion, constitute a decisive moment in furthering the precision and nihilistic radicality of the hermeneutic thesis of art as the setting into work of truth? Or, more simply: what does the 'Sant'Ivo experience' have to do with the hermeneutic defence of the truth of art and with the possibility of orienting oneself amongst the many meanings that it can take on and in fact has taken on?

The first step towards clarifying this connection is, as we have seen, the Gadamerian critique of aesthetic consciousness and also of its social equivalent, the museum.[15] All the same, as long as one confines oneself to declaring that it is not only 'aesthetic consciousness' that features in the contemplation of the work of art, but that there also occurs an encounter with truth (whether in Bloch's overly romantic prophetic sense, or as the truth of other historical worlds, or of other personal interpretations of the world) that transforms whoever is implicated in it, it seems that one remains within the bounds of that pluralistic philosophy of culture which in preceding chapters seemed to be still too characteristically metaphysical to be considered genuinely faithful to the ontological inspiration that lies at the basis of twentieth-century hermeneutics. And accordingly, neither could such a theory do justice to what has seemed to us to be the meaning of the 'Sant'Ivo experience' taken here as emblematic of the questions to which the aesthetics current in standard hermeneutic theory is unable to respond.

But again: if not this – if not an enquiry into the truth of the work as an opening of historical worlds, as a prophecy, a document, or simply a change of perspective – then what is to be done? Once again, we must return to (what are for us) the 'canonical texts' of hermeneutics: to be precise, not to the essay on 'The Origin of the Work of Art' to which we have already referred, but to a lecture that Heidegger gave in the same year, 'Hölderlin and the Essence of Poetry' – all the while keeping in mind the comments on the poets found in *Holzwege* and in the later *On the Way to Language*.[16] The lecture is a veritable *summa* of themes that we have tackled in this chapter, and provides some valuable indications that Heidegger himself did not develop in the sense that interests us here, but that can legitimately be taken up and used in the present context. Above all, we come away from this lecture with two points on which Heidegger's critique does not generally fix its attention.[17] Hölderlin is chosen by Heidegger in order to speak of the essence of poetry because, in distinction from other poets in whose work this essence unfolds, he is the 'poet of the poet'. 'Hölderlin's poetry was borne on by the poetic vocation to write expressly of the essence of poetry.'[18] This theme is very dear to Heidegger and is repeated at the beginning of the essay 'What are Poets for?', which takes its title from a verse by Hölderlin, although it goes on to deal with Rilke, who is also considered a poet of poetry inasmuch as he sings in the time of privation (the verse from Hölderlin in fact runs: 'Wozu Dichter in dürftiger Zeit?' 'What are poets for in a destitute time?'). In the main, Heidegger's critique sets aside this initial justification of the choice of Hölderlin (or Rilke), almost as though it were purely rhetorical, and moves directly to consider the significance of his reading of the texts for an understanding of the destiny of that epoch of destitution which is the epoch of metaphysics. But what is most important is simply the observation that the poets to which the philosopher can turn, today in the epoch of the end of metaphysics, are the poets that speak of the essence (the *Wesen*: the historico-ontological destiny, not the eternal nature) of poetry. By this I mean that while Heidegger's discourse does not always remain faithful to this assumption in every detail (above all in *Holzwege* and *On the Way to Language*), what he reads in the poets is by and large and fundamentally an ensemble of ideas on poetry, on the destiny of poets, on the artist's condition – not eternal, but situated, 'in a time of destitution'.[19] And – a second point that seems particularly significant for the question of secularization that interests us here – the condition of the poet is defined primarily as that of an intermediary between gods and people; but being an intermediary is not an easy function to define: 'The poet himself stands between the former – the Gods, and the latter – the people. He is one who has been cast out.' It is for this reason, he seems to believe, that Hölderlin poetizes on poetry: not 'for lack of cosmic substance' but 'because he reaches out with poetic thought into the foundation and the midst of being'. All this holds of the poet in the new time that Hölderlin founds (and does not simply mirror): it is the time 'of the gods that have fled and of the gods still to come'.[20]

As I said, it is not my intention, at least not here, to draw any more than a few preliminary indications from this text of Heidegger's; indeed it is merely to underline how, with regard to the problems presented by the 'Sant'Ivo experience', there are points raised in these pages that are not generally given enough consideration. What I have in mind is not only the fact that Hölderlin is read as a poet's poet, with all that this might mean for the 'self-reflexivity' (the critical awareness of the condition of the artist, of his languages etc.) of the early twentieth century, but also the fact that there may be a decisive link between the historico-ontological essence of poetry and the 'religious' function of the poet as the intermediary between people and gods, his singing in the moment of the absence of the ancient gods and of the god to come. All this, to adopt an attitude that we saw in the previous chapter when speaking of the facility with which certain contemporary philosophers use religious 'metaphors' without justifying them and without considering their concrete historical and doctrinal weight, is generally attributed to a certain Heideggerian 'romanticism': if he speaks of gods, it is because he is speaking of poets, and above all of a poet like Hölderlin who is deeply rooted in a classicist's nostalgia for Greece and in a certain vision of Christianity in its relation to ancient mythology . . . Once again, we are back with the questions raised in the 'System-Programme' (which we can hear echoing throughout these pages from Heidegger), issues from which 'modern' aesthetics has now liberated itself and that in Heidegger must be read and interpreted, indeed demystified, just to clarify his conception of metaphysics and its crisis . . .

In contrast to so reductive a vision of these themes (the poetry of poetry, the gods departed and that still to come) the hermeneutic endeavour to look at art independently of aestheticist perspectives and in the light of a conception of the work as an event of truth must develop a new sensitivity to two questions: the truth of art that philosophy must seek to understand is less what the artists and poets say (a path that culminates in banal 'prose versions' of their works), than the ontological significance for the history of the meaning of Being that can be perceived in the destiny of art and poetry in the epoch of the end of metaphysics. And poetry invites us to regard this epoch as an epoch of departed gods and of a (very problematic) anticipation of a god that is to come; in short as an epoch in which the problem of secularization is central.

In this way, there are really only two directions marked out for the aesthetic reflection inspired by hermeneutics to go. Nonetheless, simply to indicate these directions is already to raise some substantial issues on which, in conclusion and with no pretence to being systematic, I shall try to shed some light.

In the first place, if the interpretation of Heidegger's emphasis on the 'poetry of poetry' that I have proposed is valid, aesthetic philosophy will have to come to terms with the truth of art above all by addressing the significance for the destiny of Being of the social constitution of art in our epoch; after all, it is relatively uninteresting, and often entirely vacuous, to believe that Heidegger and hermeneutics urge us to try to extract philosophical theses from poetry, literature and the figurative arts. Moreover, to move in the direction of a historico-destinal ontology of art, it would be necessary to enquire further into the reasons behind Heidegger's decision to concentrate only on the opening of truth that is given in the work of art, and not on the other forms of the occurrence of the true named in the passage from 'The Origin of the Work of Art' to which we referred earlier. On first inspection, the reasons for this choice are clearly those which we believe we identified earlier (in Chapter 2). But it is probable that they are reducible to a more radical reason on which they depend, namely, the peculiarly central position that art assumes with respect to other forms of culture in the epoch of metaphysics and its end, that is, in modernity. The emphasis on art and the figure of the artist is a phenomenon in many respects peculiar to the modern age and it culminates as such in Romanticism, with its links to the Kantian theory of genius and to the need for a new mythology that is expressed in texts such as the 'System-Programme'.

Now this fully fledged mythicization of the figure of the artist can only be understood in the framework of a culture in which religion is substituted for art, at least (but this too is significant)

for the 'cultured classes' – a substitution which corresponds to the
emptying of the sacred that takes place in the modern age and
which entails, amongst other things, a loss (in Hegelian terms) of
the 'substantiality' of art. This is expressed in the increasing
remoteness of 'high' art from the perspective of the masses, who
remain prisoner of the kitsch which for its part seems, paradoxically and in caricature, to be a realization of the 'new mythology'
dreamed of by the Romantics. The most critical and 'militant' of
aesthetics, such as that of Adorno, can only oppose kitsch with an
avant-gardist affirmation of the purity of art that changes system-
atically into aphasia.[21] By contrast, aesthetics of a hermeneutic
inspiration shows itself to be more attentive to the social existence
of art, and even to the more problematic aspects of 'mass' art such
as rock music.[22]

It is above all in this last-named direction that it seems one
must go (not just of rock, obviously, but of the social significance
of art), although one must be aware of the ever impending risk of
finding oneself, in the rush to legitimize the new 'reproducible'
arts, confusing the truth of the work with the 'narcotic' power of
its commercial success.

The aestheticization that, with reason, many identify as a
characteristic feature of postmodern social existence,[23] has moreover and indeed above all a meaning linked to the history of late
modernity as the history of the weakening of Being. In the
preceding chapters we have tried to show that the adoption of a
nihilistic interpretation of modernity also provides criteria of
evaluation and orientation, primarily in the area of ethics. Will
this also be the case for aesthetics? We can at least be sure that a
conception of art inspired by the ontologico-hermeneutic nihilism
that we have tried to outline will not close its eyes to the
transformations that aesthetic experience has undergone and is
undergoing still in late-industrial societies. It is not a case of
insisting that the search for the truth of art be confined exclusively
to the traditional 'high' places, but of looking in addition, indeed
primarily, at the pervasive aesthetic character presently leaving its
mark on the worlds of commerce and information, and on the
whole of collective life. Its defence against being purely and simply
an apology for what already exists will lie in the principles that it
can derive from its own nihilistic inspiration and in particular

from the recognition of the link that the phenomenon of seculari-zation preserves between aesthetic experience and the religious tradition. In the precinct of this proximity may in all likelihood be found also that ensemble of phenomena of identification and of experiences of community that one finds today in certain forms of youth art (from the 'communitarian' feeling that one has at big rock concerts to the collective identity that groups of fans of the same kind of music form among themselves; punks and suchlike). If we said that the limit between 'what is of worth' and what is not in these experiences is signalled by their greater or lesser fidelity to the guiding thread of nihilism (the reduction of violence, the weakening of strong and aggressive identities, the acceptance of the other, to the point of charity) would this not be a faithful interpretation of the meaning of the nihilistic vocation of hermeneutics?

But all these are no more than examples of themes that an aesthetics of nihilist-hermeneutic inspiration would have to treat more extensively, more analytically and at greater length than it is possible to do here. Above all, the developments inspired by the 'Sant'Ivo experience' have only been mentioned in the briefest terms. It is probable that, as we have already had occasion to observe, secularization establishes between art and religion a complex relation of reciprocal action. The inessentialness that has overtaken certain manifestations of contemporary art (which often appeals only to a public of specialists, of artists involved in the same work, or of dealers who exploit its lasting cult value and thereby, very remotely, its connections with religion) may well be explained by the fact that secularization began and has been lived as the abandonment of any lingering illusion over the capacity and the duty of art to serve as a 'new mythology', a rational religion, in short, as a place in which a society or determinate social group recognize themselves and their shared convictions. Secularization, nonetheless, plainly consists in the fact that there is no longer a single shared horizon, whereupon the experience of art even as mythology and rational religion is essentially a plural experience.[24] Might the awareness of the derivational link between art and religion not also impinge in some way upon present-day forms of religious experience? If art can rediscover its own essentiality by becoming aware of its own constitution as secularized religion, religion could find in this connection a reason to think of itself in terms that are less dogmatic and disciplinarian, and more 'aesthetic', more in line with that third age, the 'age of the spirit', which may well have been one of the ideas that inspired the 'System-Programme'. We are at that point once again, and there is no reason to be ashamed of it.

Appendix 1

The Truth of Hermeneutics

How does hermeneutic ontology speak about truth? This question must address the widely held suspicion that the philosophical position of hermeneutics is relativist, anti-intellectualist, irrationalist and, at best, traditionalist. For it lacks that instance of truth which the metaphysical tradition (we use the expression here in Heidegger's sense) has always thought in terms of evidence[1] (the incontrovertible givenness of the thing, fostered by a suitable strategy of approach) and the correspondence of the proposition to the (evidence of the) thing and how things are. The Heideggerian critique of the notion of truth as correspondence seems to deprive hermeneutics of this instance, and even to make it impossible for hermeneutics to 'save the phenomena', to acknowledge the experience of truth that we all have, whether it be in openly defending the validity of an assertion or in putting forward a rational critique of the existing order (a mythical tradition, an *idolum fori*, an unjust social structure), or, above all, in correcting a false opinion and so passing from appearance to truth. Without some idea of evidence, *and thus* of correspondence, is it still possible to secure these applications of the notion of truth, without which thought seems to abdicate its vocation?

One can reply to such a question only by trying to reconstruct, or perhaps to construct, at least in good part, the positive terms of a hermeneutic conception of truth on the basis of and beyond the 'destruction' of truth as correspondence performed by Heidegger. To begin with, however, let us recall (here too, perhaps, correcting some of the implicit but nonetheless influential misapprehensions of Heidegger's interpreters) the essential motives for Heidegger's rejection of the notion of truth as correspondence. The misapprehension we are concerned to put right is that in *Being and Time* Heidegger looks for a more adequate description of the meaning of Being and of the idea of truth – as if the notion of Being as presence handed down to us by metaphysics, and the corresponding notion of truth as the correspondence of proposition to thing, were partial, incomplete, or somehow inadequate and therefore false, descriptions of Being as it is *really* given and of the experience of truth as it *really* occurs. That this might not be Heidegger's intention is, from the beginning of the work, less than clear. However, it may be appreciated well enough if one reflects that such an intention could only be contradictory, even solely in light of the features at play within truth as correspondence. But with the evolution of Heidegger's work after *Being and Time*, it becomes clear that his ontology cannot in any way be taken for a kind of existentially phrased neo-Kantianism (where the structure of reason and its a priori have fallen into the thrownness and finitude of Dasein's project) and therefore also that his objection to the conception of truth as correspondence is not based on its inadequacy as a faithful description of the experience of truth. For with the acknowledgement of inadequacy it emerges that one cannot keep to a conception of truth as correspondence, since this implies a conception of Being as *Grund*, as an insuperable first principle that reduces all questioning to silence. Moreover, it is precisely the meditation on the insufficiency of the idea of truth as the correspondence of judgement to thing that has set us on the path of Being as event. Granted, to say that 'Being is event' – as Heidegger pointedly never did, but as one is almost obliged to do when speaking of him and his philosophy in that inevitable, ambiguous and distortive relation to the language of metaphysics that led to the interruption of *Being and Time* and which Heidegger in some sense accepts, beginning, after the *Kehre*, to speak in metaphysical terms again, reworking them with the resigned distortion of the *Verwindung*[2] – to say that Being is event is itself apparently to offer a descriptive proposition that claims to be 'adequate'. But only those who bow before the ontological implications of the principle of non-contradiction will be satisfied by this kind of superficial remark that one often finds in the 'winning' arguments of metaphysics (the argument against scepticism is a typical example). They do not persuade anyone to change their view, however, and above all they do not allow for any further advance in thinking (which, within the horizon of the ontology of the principle of identity and non-contradiction, appears committed simply to a colossal work of tautology). In general, Heidegger has taught us to refuse the untroubled identification of the structures of Being with the structures of our historical grammar and of language as it is in fact given; thus also with the immediate identification of Being with that which is sayable without performative contradictions in the context of the language that we happen to speak.

To say that Being is event means somehow to pronounce, still in the language of metaphysics, consciously accepted and *verwunden*, the ultimate proposition of metaphysics (whose accomplishment and conclusion, end, is nihilism – which is this same proposition). It is, albeit experienced in other terms, the same process of unfoundation [*sfondamento*] by taking the logic of foundation to its extremes as that which Nietzsche 'described' with the proposition 'God is dead.'

It would not be slipshod to reconstruct all of the second Heidegger's thought as an elaboration of this contradiction, whereby the *Kehre* is entirely resolved – dissolved – into *Verwindung*, the resigned resumption-distortion-acceptance of metaphysics and of nihilism. We recall this ensemble of problems here only in order to remind ourselves that, in attempting to construct a positive hermeneutic conception of the experience of truth beyond the pure and simple destruction of truth as correspondence, we must allow ourselves to be guided by the authentic demands that motivated Heidegger in that destruction – motives which are not reducible to the search for a description that is truer because more adequate but which have, instead, to do with the impossibility of still thinking Being as *Grund*, as a first principle that can be given only to the precise contemplation, panoramic but soundless, of *noûs*. As I hope to show, returning to the true motives behind Heidegger's critique of the notion of truth correspondence is crucial if one is to overcome the aporias that seem, and not only in the view of its critics, to threaten the hermeneutic conception of truth. Such a conception, which finds its point of departure in what Heidegger calls 'opening', will avoid the risks to which critics of hermeneutics have drawn our attention, sometimes with good reason (the risks of irrationalism, relativism and traditionalism), only insofar as it remains genuinely faithful to the demands that motivated Heidegger's destruction; these aimed to 'respond' to the meaning of Being as event, and not to propose a more adequate conception of truth.

This guiding thread will also help us to resolve, or at least to articulate more productively, a problem that post-Heideggerian hermeneutics does not seem until now to have posed in the right terms: the question of the relation between truth as opening and truth as correspondence; or, which is in many senses the same thing, between truth in philosophy (and in the human sciences) and truth in the positive sciences. Every reader of *Truth and Method*, and perhaps also of Gadamer's later works, will know that it is not clear how far Gadamer intends, in that work, to claim the capacity for truth *also* for the human sciences founded upon interpretation, or whether he wishes to propose this 'model' of truth as valid in general for every experience of truth, and thus for the experimental sciences too. Either way, it seems that this 'obscurity' in Gadamer may be easily explained by noting that, at least in *Truth and Method*, the Heidegger to which he makes most constant and wide-ranging reference is the Heidegger of *Being and Time*.[3] Now, on the basis of *Being and Time*, one can say that the simple presence to which both banal everydayness and scientific objectivism may be reduced, albeit in different terms, arises from a partial attitude that cannot serve as the only model for thinking Being. Inauthentic thought, which already in *Being and Time* is the ontology that must be destroyed and which will later become the metaphysics that forgets Being in favour of beings thought as simple presence, is that which (for reasons that appear at first to be linked to the sedimentation of Dasein in worldly commerce; and which, in the Heidegger of the *Kehre*, will then have to do with the very destiny of Being and its epochal essence) thinks not only worldly entities, but Being itself, and Dasein too, according to the model of simple presence and the objectivity of objects. To avoid both inauthenticity and the careless and forgetful distortions of metaphysics, it would seem, therefore, that one must simply resist this unwarranted extension of the model of the simple presence of entities and objects to Being itself. Gadamer does not seem to go any further than this in his criticism of modern scientism in *Truth and Method*. Such scientism is, for him, not the inevitable outcome of metaphysics; less still is it a fact bound up with the destiny and history of metaphysics, as it clearly is for Heidegger in the works after *Being and Time*. Even Rorty's thesis in *Philosophy and the Mirror of Nature*, in which he distinguishes between 'epistemology' and 'hermeneutics' in terms that may well refer back to correspondence and opening,[4] seems to be a reformulation (albeit too 'urbanized', like that of Gadamer) of a position whose basis may be traced in *Being and Time*. Epistemology is the construction of a body of rigorous knowledge and the solution of problems in the light of paradigms that lay down the rules for the verification of propositions; to be sure, these rules do not necessarily imply that whoever follows them gives a truthful account of how things are, but at least they do not exclude it. Moreover, they allow a conception of science and a scientific practice to survive that are for the most part in harmony with the traditional metaphysical vision of the correspondence between proposition and thing. Hermeneutics, by contrast, unfolds in the encounter with different paradigmatic horizons. Resisting evaluation on the basis of any correspondence (to rules or, ultimately, to the thing), such horizons manifest themselves as 'poetic' proposals of other worlds, of the institution of different rules – within which another 'epistemology' is in force.

We shall pursue here neither the suggestions nor, above all, the problems arising from Rorty's hypothesis, which are, it seems, for the most part common to the Gadamerian perspective as well, although Gadamer himself has always said very little on the subject of the relation between knowledge in the interpretative sciences and knowledge in the hard or natural sciences. One relevant difference between his position and that of Rorty may lie in the way that Gadamer (above all in the essays in *Reason in the Age of Science*[5]) confers a kind of supremacy on knowledge in the human sciences, on the moral plane at least. The natural sciences, with their inevitable link with technology and their tendency towards specialization (not only in knowledge, but also in the pursuit of ever more specific ends, possibly in conflict with the general interests of society), must be 'legitimized' by a thinking which relates them back to the *logos*, to the common consciousness expressed in the natural-historic language of a society and in its shared culture, whose continuity – even, it has to be said, in the sense of a *critical* reconstruction – is assured precisely by the human sciences and by philosophy in particular. In the terminology of *Being and Time* (and then of 'Vom Wesen der Wahrheit'), the opening (which occurs in language, and in its founding events, like the work of art spoken of in an essay in *Holzwege*[6]) is truth in its most original sense, which also serves as a point of reference for the legitimation of truth as correspondence in the sciences. The latter, however, insofar as they specialize via the construction of artificial languages, 'do not think', as first Heidegger and then Gadamer after him have said.[7] As for Rorty, he takes up what seems to be a more radical position than that of Gadamer in which there is no trace of the distinction between natural and human sciences: each form of knowledge may be in a hermeneutic 'phase' or an epistemological one, according to whether it is experiencing a 'normal' or a 'revolutionary' period, to use Kuhn's terms.[8] However, this excludes any possible hierarchy between the knowledges, or any privileged place for human rationality in general, such as Gadamer's *logos*-language (and common sense, charged with history). Yet just how radical is this difference between Gadamer and Rorty? Both, it seems (at least insofar as Gadamer too refuses to follow Heidegger in speaking of a history of Being), relate truth as correspondence back to truth as opening, understood either (in Gadamer) as an historico-cultural horizon shared by a community that speaks the same language, and within which specific rules of verification and validation are in force, or as a paradigm that, without necessarily being identified with a linguistic community or a cultural universe (but equally without necessarily excluding such an identification), nonetheless contains the rules for the solution of its own internal problems, and, as a whole, manifests itself as a foundation which is not in its turn founded, not even by that historical continuity which still seems to be operative in Gadamer; for whom, however, the problem ultimately remains the same as with Rorty, since he too regards the historical continuity that legitimizes the opening (and which prevents its reduction to a relatively arbitrary and casual paradigm, to one lacking any further justification, as in Rorty – unless it were justified in hackneyed vitalistic terms) as nonetheless a limited community in that it does not permit, at least not explicitly, the passage to the limit that would bind it to humanity in general. There is, for Rorty, but in the end probably for Gadamer as well, a certain 'Weberian' relativism in place: one can speak of truth in the sense of conformity with rules, given with the opening itself, only within an historical-cultural opening or paradigm. At the same time, the opening as such cannot be said to be 'true' on the basis of criteria of conformity, but is (at least for Gadamer, explicitly) original truth since it institutes the horizons within which all verification and falsification is possible. Our 'hermeneutic' experience of the opening is more or less explicitly 'aesthetic'; this is clear in Rorty, who conceives the encounter with other paradigms as an encounter with a new system of metaphors or a poetic creation.[9] Not by chance does Gadamer himself begin *Truth and Method* by affirming the capacity of art to convey truth, except that in Gadamer the encounter with other openings of the world constitutive of interpretation is aesthetic experience only to the extent that the latter is thought fundamentally in historical terms, as an integration, or better still an 'application', in the present of a call whose provenance lies in the past.

In fact, it is to Gadamer more than to Rorty that we should turn for an articulation of the hermeneutic doctrine of truth as opening; even if it is precisely in him that the problems entailed by such a conception become clear, forcing us to return to Heidegger, to his thought as it develops after *Being and Time*, and to what seem to us to be the fundamental demands already motivating the critique of truth as correspondence in that work.

If it is not (thought as) the incontrovertible givenness of an object held in a clear and distinct idea and adequately described in a proposition that faithfully reflects that idea – which is (perhaps) possible only within a horizon, an opening to the thing that institutes every possible criterion of conformity of the proposition (to the thing, or at least to the rules of language) – then the truth of the opening can, it seems, only be thought on the basis of the metaphor of dwelling. At bottom, this is the case not only for Gadamer, but for Rorty as well: I can do epistemology, I can formulate propositions that are valid according to certain rules, only on the condition that I dwell in a determinate linguistic universe or paradigm. It is 'dwelling' that is the first condition of my saying the truth. But I cannot describe it as a universal, structural and stable condition, for historical experience (and lately that of the history of science as well) evinces the irreducibility of heterogeneous paradigms and cultural universes, and moreover (independently of this first, and possibly problematic, reason) in order to describe the opening as a stable structure, I would need a criterion of conformity, which would then be the more original opening.

It is in terms of dwelling, therefore, that I shall speak of truth as opening (which I call truth because, like rules regarding individual propositions, it is the first condition of every particular truth). Dwelling in the truth is, to be sure, very different from showing and simply rendering explicit what always already is. In this respect Gadamer is right when he observes that belonging to a tradition, or even in Wittgensteinian terms to a form of life, does not mean passively undergoing the imposition of a system of prejudices;[10] in certain other contemporary readings of Nietzsche this would be equivalent to the total (more or less explicit) reduction of truth to a play of forces.[11] Dwelling implies, rather, an interpretative belonging which involves both consensus and the possibility of critical activity: not for nothing, one might add (to be critical of the optimism of this conception), do modern dictatorships give an ever greater place to techniques for the organization of consensus. Dominion through consensus is more secure and more stable. Nevertheless, there is a certain difference from pure constriction established here which perhaps humanizes the exercise of despotic power. It certainly recognizes, albeit paradoxically, the decisive significance of a conscious adhesion (or at least what is taken for such) to a tradition, and the always active interpretative character of staying in a tradition. As a metaphor for speaking of hermeneutic truth, dwelling might best be understood as though one were dwelling in a library; whereas the idea of truth as correspondence conceives of knowledge of the true as the possession of an 'object' by way of an adequate representation, the truth of dwelling is by contrast the competence of the librarian who does not possess entirely, in a single act of transparent comprehension, all of the contents of all of the books amongst which he lives, nor even the first principles upon which the contents depend. One cannot compare such knowledge-possession through the command of first principles to the competence of librarianship, which knows where to look because it knows how the volumes are classified and is also acquainted with the 'subject catalogue'.

It is therefore senseless and misleading to accuse hermeneutics of being reducible to a relativism or irrationalism for which each articulation within the opening, each epistemology, would be merely the manifestation, the revelation (once again, according to a simplistic model of adequation) of that which, without any choice, always already is (such that the conflict of interpretations would be nothing but a genuine conflict between forces that have no 'argument' whatsoever to offer, other than the violence by which their predomination is secured). For thrownness in a historical opening is always inseparable from an active participation in its constitution, its creative interpretation and transformation. However, these suspicions about hermeneutics are always revived by its apparent inability to describe 'original' truth in terms of dwelling without recourse to a further metaphor rooted deeply in the metaphysical tradition; namely, that of 'community', or even, in Hegel's terms, 'beautiful ethical life' (the persistent force of this reference is still in evidence, most recently in Habermas's *Theory of Communicative Action* where the appeal to the *Lebenswelt* is thought, implicitly but quite clearly, via the ideal of an organic community characterized in terms of ethical life, and has both a normative and a foundational role). Ethical life seems to be indispensable, if hermeneutic dwelling is to include a moment of 'evidence', of the recognition of truth, without having to fall back into the model of correspondence. In other words, truth as opening also seems to involve a moment of 'recognition', a 'sensation' of incontrovertibility, of full evidence, of a result reached. In accordance with the characteristically aesthetic quality of the hermeneutic experience of truth, but plainly also with its links with pragmatism (such links as are currently promoted by Rorty are legitimized by aspects of prag-

matism in the existential analytic in *Being and Time*), this comes
to be understood as the recognition of a harmonious integration,
more than as the appropriation of a certain content via an
adequate representation. Classical doctrines of evidence as characteristic not only of certainty but also of truth have (until phenomenology) always striven to regard this sensation of integration
and achieved harmony as a sign and symptom to which the truth
of the content of experience cannot be reduced; yet they have
done so without ever producing convincing proof that this difference really existed. Nietzsche acknowledges this too, when he
invites us to doubt precisely that which appears to be most
evident, certain and indisputable. This passage (which looks like
a kind of neo-classical metaphysics: from the principle of non-
contradiction to the structure of Being; from our not being able to
say differently to Being's not being able to be differently) is
comprehensively liquidated in the hermeneutic conception of truth
as opening. The truth of the opening is not an object whose
cognitive possession may be authenticated by the sensation of
evidence, completeness and integration that we might feel in a
given moment. This integration is the original truth itself, the
condition of our being in the true on which depends the possibility
of making judgements that are true inasmuch as they are verified
in the light of rules of correspondence.

Can these complications, and the problems connected with
them, be avoided by reducing truth to merely 'secondary' truth,
to truth as correspondence, as in the end metaphysics (with the
exception of Kant) has always done? Yes, but only by 'reducing
Being to beings', in Heidegger's phrase, or in a different terminology, at the price of remaining prisoners of ideology, unable to
place any distance between it and ourselves, and of identifying the
paradigm or cultural universe into which we are thrown with the
real world *tout court*. Which, it is understood, *one cannot do*: one
cannot knowingly construct myth, one cannot (not because one
should not, but because it cannot be done) artificially assume
(after the critique of ideology, after historicism, after Nietzsche) a
'natural' attitude ... So (and this could be argued at length) the
problem of truth as opening is posed in a way from which we
cannot prescind, and, that is, as a problem of opening as truth;
for, once again, not to consider the historical-cultural (or, with

Heidegger, the ontologico-destinal) condition into which we are thrown to be a problem of truth means to take it, more or less consciously, as a brute fact, whose inevitable reduction to an effect of force (truth as 'will to power') is merely a sign of its remaining within the sphere of a metaphysics of foundations; a prisoner once more of *Grund* as the ultimate instance beyond which one does not go and which silences all questioning and thereby closes the discourse. Thus we cannot help but pose the problem of opening (why and for what reasons should we decide to take the world as being identical to our historical description of it, which in the meantime, as a result of the evolution of metaphysics into nihilism, has appeared to us *as such*?), and we cannot help but (that is we must) pose the problem of opening in terms of truth. If we do not, we shall end up still taking it to be a brute fact, a *Grund*. Yet this seems to be 'prohibited' both by the need, which can no longer be ignored after Marx, Nietzsche and Heidegger, to distinguish the opening from its articulation (the hermeneutic from the epistemological) and also, in a related fashion, because that which becomes unthinkable with the experience of the distinction between the opening and single truths (or, in other words, with the ontological difference) is precisely something like *Grund* – which becomes that which is most suspect, precisely insofar as it is presented as the ultimate instance, silencing, authoritative (and authoritarian). It was the impossibility of continuing to think Being in terms of *Grund* that inspired Heidegger's critique of truth as correspondence, which could not have been moved by the desire to find a more adequate description than that handed down by metaphysics.

Yet does this need that Heidegger raises, and which we assume here to be ineluctable, find a response in the reduction of the evidence of the givenness of the object (and of truth as correspondence) to an aesthetic experience of *fulfilment*, of harmonious integration in a community, of self-recognition in Hegelian spirit? It is not simply a matter of regarding with suspicion the aestheticism which this hermeneutic conception of the experience of truth seems necessarily to involve. Aestheticism – for in the end such is the referral of the sensation of objective evidence back to a recognition of integration in the world in which one 'dwells' and in which one feels at home, as though in beautiful ethical life – is 'suspect' only insofar as it does not bid farewell to the true as *Grund*, but seems instead to be a still more monumental and peremptory version of it. The solution to the problems and discomforts created by life in a 'society' held together only by contractual, mechanical and conventional links is not the reconstruction of an organic community; just as the recovery of a notion of virtue within a concrete historical horizon of shared values (through belonging to a common tradition) is not the solution to the subjectivist aporias in which modern rationalist ethics has issued. It is not, perhaps, by chance that the critiques moved by modern ethical rationalism, exemplified by McIntyre's reflections on ethics, conclude in the proposal of a return to a premodern morality.[12] This demonstrates a risk that is also run by the hermeneutic conception of truth. At times in Gadamer it seems to be something more than a risk. Yet in Gadamer, as in Rorty and his conception of 'conversation', there are the resources required to prevent the 'aesthetic' model which underlies the hermeneutic conception of truth from leading to aestheticist results. It is a matter of recognizing these elements while keeping in mind the proposal that, as we have said, guides the Heideggerian critique of truth as correspondence. In this way, one would also be more faithful to an 'aesthetic' model no longer thought in anachronistic classical terms. In effect, while truth as the appropriation of a thing via an adequate representation is indeed replaced in hermeneutics by truth thought as dwelling and as an aesthetic more than a cognitive-appropriative experience, this aesthetic experience is in its turn thought on the basis of its actual configuration in the epoch of the end of metaphysics to which hermeneutic ontology itself belongs. For this experience, what presents itself today as complete and well-round, boasting the harmonious conciliation and perfect interpenetration of content and form that were (thought to be) proper to art in its classical sense, is precisely and only the false work of art, kitsch. The connection between hermeneutics and aesthetics in the epoch of the end of metaphysics could also be formulated in this way: to assert the importance of aesthetic experience for truth, as does nineteenth-century hermeneutics, and moreover to offer it as a significant 'model' for a conception of truth free from the prejudices of scientism (that is, from the idea of truth as correspondence and the evidence of the object), is only possible when aesthetic experience is modified to such a degree that it loses the 'classical' characteristics with which it has been associated in the metaphysical tradition. This transformation of the aesthetic, which we must follow Heidegger in regarding as a feature of the destiny of Being, is probably matched by a radical transformation of cognitive experience in the sciences, to the point where (but it is only a hypothesis here) the proposal of aesthetic experience as a 'model of truth' might no longer appear foreign or opposed to the self-knowledge concurrently reaching maturity in the sciences.

The critique of the idea of truth as correspondence, then, leads hermeneutics to conceive of truth on the model of dwelling and aesthetic experience. But this experience still tends to be presented according to classical images of integration, harmony and well-roundness corresponding to the manifestation of art in the epoch of metaphysics (and thus also in the epoch of truth as correspondence); if hermeneutics gives in to this tendency, it will end up by opposing truth as correspondence with nothing more than an idealization of the beautiful ethical life. Instead of escaping the authority of *Grund* (and its forgetful identification of Being and beings), this would merely reassert an even more monumental foundationalism, one that could express itself in the pure and simple identification of the opening with the brute factuality of a certain form of life not open to discussion, and which shows itself only in its holding as the horizon of every possible judgement. A more accurate recognition of the aesthetic experience that serves as a model here and a radical fidelity to the purpose behind the (Heideggerian) critique of truth as correspondence lead instead to a different outcome.[13] First, they lead to a distancing from the emphasis that metaphysical thought has always placed upon the subjective sensation of certainty, taken as a sign of truth. Regardless of every effort to the contrary, it seems impossible, after Nietzsche, still to think of clear and distinct ideas as the model for truth, or of the experience of the true as the incontrovertible certainty of consciousness before a given content. The Nietzschean 'school of suspicion', surely, can lead only to a demystification so radical as to demystify suspicion itself. Such an outcome, however, is not equivalent, as many tend to believe, to a recuperation pure and simple of the evidence proper to consciousness, this side of any suspicion. If hermeneutics wishes to be faithful to the intentions (and good reasons) underlying the Heideggerian critique of truth as correspondence, it cannot simply offer another explanation of the experience of evidence, referring the sensation of fullness, satisfaction and stillness back to a cause distinct from the manifestation of the thing in its simple presence – for example, to the sense of integration in a community thought as Hegelian beautiful ethical life, which to all intents and purposes functions as *Grund*, all the more peremptory and compelling in the absence of the distance guaranteed by objectification. (Should it not be said that, with respect to the organic unity of mythical consciousness, the metaphysical reduction of Being to beings is already a first announcement of the ontological difference?) For hermeneutics it is a matter, rather, of fully recognizing the link between the evidence of consciousness itself and metaphysics, whose history comprises the manner in which truth is given as a clear and distinct idea and as incontrovertible certainty. In this case too, as in general with all elements of the history of metaphysics, thinking cannot delude itself that it can perform a genuine overcoming. It must instead work at a *Verwindung*, a resumption and distortion,[14] which here will mean maintaining the model of correspondence as a secondary moment of the experience of truth.

After Nietzsche, but at bottom simply after Kant (whose transcendental foundation already places particular truths and the correspondence of propostions on a secondary level), we no longer think of truth as the correspondence of a proposition to how things are. Such truth as correspondence, and even as incontrovertible evidence experienced in the certainty of consciousness, is only a secondary moment within the sphere of the experience of truth, which is revealed as such precisely with the maturation of metaphysics towards its completion; for example, with the advent of modern experimental science and its far-reaching technological consequences, with the transformation of the scientific project into a social undertaking of gigantic proportions and irreducible complexity – which render *de facto* irrelevant that mythical moment of discovery and conscious certainty on the model of which metaphysics constructed its idea of truth. Just as, going back to aesthetic experience, to conceive the encounter with the work of art in terms of the classically perfect identification

between content and form, and the completeness and definitive
. quality of the work, is anachronistic, illusory and in the end
positively kitsch (nowadays only merchandise promoted in adver-
tising is presented in this way), so still to think of the 'eureka' of
a scientist in the laboratory as the principal moment, as the very
model for the significance of the experience of truth, is ideological
and mystificatory. Perhaps it is from there that the experience of
truth *begins*, as one sets out from certainty on a voyage to discover
the conditions which render it possible (or perhaps belie it), and
which are never given once and for all in evidence that is incisive,
simultaneous, exhaustive and comparable to the initial moment in
which a content is 'installed' as incontrovertible.

To the *Erklärung*, to positive-scientific 'explanation', employing
perfectly evident relations to subsume a single case under a general
law that is itself given as evident, hermeneutics does not oppose a
Verstehen that, as a lived experience of affinity and common
belonging, reproduces at the level of vitalistic immediacy the same
'silencing' authority of objective evidence. Instead, it sets in
opposition what Heidegger might call an *Erörterung*,[15] a unfounding [*sfondante*[16]] 'collocation' that has indeed many of the traits
of aesthetic experience, but as it is given at the end of metaphysics
and as a moment of its 'overcoming' in the form of a *Verwindung*.
The research opened up by Kant on the conditions of possibility
of physics as a science finds here perhaps, and maybe paradoxically, its consummation: physics as a science, or in general modern
technical science as it is set out in the world of *Ge-Stell*, in totally
organized society, is possible only on the condition of no longer
thinking truth on the model of the evidence proper to consciousness. The modern scientific project itself heralds the consummation of that model, the relegation of truth as correspondence to a
second level, ultimately the ever more emphatic divarication
between the real – as that which is given in the immediacy of a
compelling intuition – and the true, as that which is established
only by virtue of its being situated within an unfounding horizon.

All of which, naturally, one would have to argue in greater
detail, reconstructing the rising self-consciousness of the sciences
over the nineteenth and twentieth centuries, for example, with
particular reference to the debate on realism and conventionalism
up to and including some of the most recent contributions (such

as Feyerabend's methodological anarchism, of course, but also the renewed interest in 'realism' and its various significations[17]).

From the point of view of hermeneutics – to which I confine my attention in this essay – the features of the *Erörterung* as an alternative to the metaphysical 'model of truth' as correspondence (and to its variations in the sense of the organic community) are delineated more clearly if, while keeping in mind the character-istics of late-modern aesthetic experience, one reflects further on the metaphor of dwelling (which is, after all, central to many of Heidegger's writings). To speak more specifically of dwelling in a library is, however, merely to highlight a feature common to all dwelling, namely, the introduction of oneself not into a natural space conceived ultimately as abstract and geometrical, but into a landscape bearing the marks of a tradition. The library in which late-modern man lives, and within which lies his experience of truth, is, to use Borges's expression, a 'library of Babel'. The elements for this specification of the concept of *Erörterung* can already be traced in the distinction Heidegger underscores in *Being and Time* between tradition as *Tradition* and tradition as *Über-lieferung* (understood as the active inheritance of the past as an open possibility, not as a rigidly determined and determining schema[18]). What constitutes the truth of the particular truths given in propositions that 'correspond' (to the thing, but above all to the rules of verification) is the reference back to conditions of possibility which cannot in their turn be stated in a proposition that corresponds, but which are instead given as an endless network of references constituted by the multiple voices of the *Über-lieferung*, of the handing down (not necessarily from the past), that echo through the language in which those propositions are formulated. These voices – and this is a specifically modern experience, thereby making the link between the giving of truth as *Erörterung* and the ending of metaphysics impossible to avoid – speak as an irreducible multiplicity, resisting every attempt to draw them back to a unity (as still capable of being given in the form of a content that can be grasped in a single look and stated in a proposition that corresponds). Does not the closed and definitive system of the Kantian categories crumble also, and indeed precisely, by reason of discovering of the multiplicity of cultural universes, and thus the irreducible plurality of a priori conditions of different knowledges? This multiplicity, however, would remain only a factual given with no philosophical significance, if philosophy for its part did not link it to the discovery of the temporality constitutive of Being, as happens in Heidegger. The irreducible multiplicity of cultural universes becomes philosophically relevant only when seen in the light of the mortality constitutive of Dasein, which confers on the *Über-lieferung* not the character of a confused superposition of perspectives that disturb the apprehension of the thing as it is, but the dignity of the *Ge-Schick*, of the giving of Being as the handing down of openings which vary from time to time, as do the generations of humanity. This is to be kept in mind, even beyond the letter of Heidegger's text, in order to understand how it is that the tradition within which truths as corresponding propositions are introduced and acquire their most authentic truth is not only Babelic as an irreducible multiplicity of voices, but also has a 'fallen' character that marks it as a dissolutive source compared with a giving of Being as simple presence. This aspect of the *Über-lieferung*, which brings together the sense of transmission and the more specific sense of handing down and provenance, is recognized explicitly here in order to avoid yet another metaphysical equivocality that can be seen in all versions of hermeneutics as pure relativism – versions that take hermeneutics purely as a philosophy of the irreducible multiplicity of perspectives. Now, in Heideggerian hermeneutics, the irreducible multiplicity of perspectives is opened by the mortality constitutive of Dasein, which finds itself always already thrown into a project, into a language, a culture, that it *inherits*. First and foremost, the awareness of the multiplicity of perspectives, of the cultural universes and of the a priori that make experience of the world possible, is *inheritance*. The conception of truth as dwelling in the Library of Babel is not a true description of the experience of truth that would in the end replace as false the metaphysical conception of truth as correspondence. It is, rather, the outcome of the unfolding of metaphysics as the reduction of Being to presence, of its culmination in techno-science, and of the consequent dissolution of the very idea of reality in the multiplicity of interpretations. Situating truths, propositions that 'correspond', within truth as opening does not simply mean suspending their ultimate cogency within a multiplicity of perspectives that renders them possible (and also shows them to be *merely* possible). This, as far as one can see, might stand as a description of the deconstructionist version of hermeneutics proposed by Jacques Derrida. Instead, the hermeneutic *Erörterung* situates truth against the background [*sfondo*] of the irreducible multiplicity of voices that make them possible; but it experiences this situation as a response, in its turn, to a call that comes from the *Über-lieferung*, and which keeps this unfoundation [*sfondamento*] from simply being confusion, or at the very least arbitrariness.[19]

This seems to be the only way to pose not only the problem of truth as opening (truths as propositions that correspond need a horizon that renders them possible), but also the problem of opening as truth (the supporting horizon cannot be reduced to a brute fact, insuperable and endowed with the same peremptory authority as metaphysical *Grund*). The multiplicity of voices against the background of which alone single truths acquire authentic truth is not, in its turn, an ultimate structure given as true in the place of Being as unity, *arche* and foundation. It is, rather, provenance: Being, which in metaphysics is given in the form of presence opened out to the point where it dissolves in the objectivity of the objects of techno-science and in the subjectivity of the modern subject, itself always close to turning into an object (of measurement, manipulation etc.), is given today as multiplicity, temporality, mortality. To recognize this giving as an event, and not as the unveiling of an already-given, peremptory and ineluctable structure, means to find in the multiplicity of voices in which the a priori is dissolved not only an anarchic confusion, but the call of a *Ge-schick*, of a destiny that no longer has the characteristics of metaphysical ground just because it consists in the dissolution of ground. The *Ge-schick* retains something of metaphysical *Grund* and its capacity for legitimation; but only in the paradoxical, nihilistic form of a vocation for dissipation that cannot, precisely for this reason, present itself as compelling in a metaphysical sense, but which nonetheless represents a possible rationality for thought, a possible 'truth of the opening'. Thus, in the sphere of this dissolutionary destiny of Being, the succession of scientific paradigms and science's growing awareness of its own historically situated character are not resolved by the substitution of a relativistic metaphysics for the realist metaphysics of the tradition (a move that twentieth-century thought has manifestly often desired). The divarication of the *true* and the *real*, which seems to be one of the most striking consequences of the development of modern science (the entities of which it speaks bear increasingly little resemblance to the 'things' of everyday experience; partly because many of these entities are themselves the products of technology), would acquire the sense here of an aspect of the history of the completion and dissolution of metaphysics. At the end of this history Being is given as that which *is not*, at least not in the sense of an object, of present and stable reality; like the opening that makes possible particular truths as propositions that correspond to the given, while yet explicitly withdrawing from any kind of appropriable susceptibility to being stated. The conquest of the true would therefore be a path leading away from the real as the immediate pressure of the given, the incontrovertible imposition of the *in itself*, the evidence of which would thus appear, to use an example from psychoanalysis, increasingly like the fascination of the imaginary and its games of identification, from which, in Lacan's terminology, one can only withdraw via a passage to the level of the symbolic.[20]

The unfounding horizon within which, from this perspective, particular truths (even as scientific statements that 'correspond') acquire their authentic truth, that is come to be 'founded', would be neither the historically determined paradigm that contains the rules of their formulation and yet brooks no further interrogation (like a form of life which legitimizes itself by the very fact of its existence), nor merely the disordered multiplicity of paradigms that, once evoked by philosophy and the history of ideas, would serve to suspend the claims of particular truths to definitive status. To stand in the opening is not to undergo a harmonious (traditionalist, conservative) integration into a canon that is received and shared on the basis of an organic community; nor is it the pure relativist-historicist detachment of the blasé (which Mannheim regarded in *Ideology and Utopia* as the only possible point of view not limited by ideology,[21] and which is taken up not by the Marxian proletariat, but by the European intellectual formed in and by the knowledge of many cultural universes). Rather, one gets back to truth as opening by taking the unfoundation as destiny. If it is true that the developments of science evince a growing divarication of the true from the real, then this destiny means that the divarication attests not only to the insuperable historical relativity of the paradigms, with all the consequences – theoretical too – that this involves (first amongst which is the permanent temptation to scepticism), but also to Being's vocation for the reduction and dissolution of strong characteristics. This presents itself as a possible guiding thread for interpretations, choices, and even moral options, far beyond the pure and simple affirmation of the plurality of paradigms.[22]

What remains in this perspective of the evidence of the object and the 'traditional' notion of truth as correspondence? Paradoxically, but not excessively so, what is enhanced here is the *critical* function of truth, its taking the form of a leap into the *logoi*, an ever renewed passage 'from here to there', to use the Platonic expression – inasmuch as even the consciousness of evidence is continually re-interrogated regarding its conditions, forever drawn back into the horizon of the opening that constitutes its permanent unfoundation. The sensation of success and the feeling of fullness that accompanies the 'discovery' – which under the conditions of scientific research today is increasingly delegated to measurements, instrumental verifications, the establishment of continuity and 'tests' between 'objects' – if they are experienced at all any more, are relegated to the rank of secondary effects of truth, or else serve as points of departure that one must leave behind as too heavily compromised by the pressure of the 'real' (a separation that began with the distinction between primary and secondary qualities, and in general with the ideal of disinterestedness and scientific objectivity).

The growing historico-political self-awareness of science (on account of which epistemology at its best turns increasingly from the theory of knowledge, logic and the theory of scientific language towards the sociology of the scientific community) might well be numbered amongst the aspects of this transformation of the notion of truth; a notion that does not explicitly deny the ideal of correspondence, but which situates it on a second and lower level with respect to truth as opening. (Despite appearances, this does not amount to a reaffirmation of the supremacy of philosophy and of the human sciences over the natural sciences. Rorty's

distinction, recalled earlier, between 'epistemology' and 'hermeneutics' is moreover probably too schematic, drawing too rigid a
distinction between the work of the internal articulation of a
paradigm, the solution of puzzles, and the revolutionary transformation of the paradigm itself. For scientific work, even from the
standpoint of Popperian falsificationism, is difficult to describe as
simply the articulation of rules given in verifying the correspondence between propositions and states of things. And on the other
hand, the institution of historical openings, of new horizons of
truth, is perhaps a less aesthetically emphatic event than Rorty
seems to think.)

Neither is the other traditional metaphysical usage of truth, in
which the universal validity of true statements is guaranteed on
the basis of the thing being given 'in person', entirely lost in the
hermeneutic reformulation of truth as opening. Here, in place of
the merely postulated universality of true propositions – always
postponed to the surreptitious identification of the 'we' of the
determinate scientific community or the specific cultural universe
(Western Europe in the eighteenth and nineteenth centuries,
ultimately) with humanity in general – there is an actual setting
into relation of particular truths with the multiplicity of perspectives constituting the network that supports them and renders
them possible. Once again, it is worth repeating that the hermeneutic conception of truth is not an affirmation of the 'local' over
the 'global', or any such 'parochial' reduction of the experience of
the true – for which statements would hold true only within a
delimited horizon, and could never aspire to a wider validity. To
open up – as Heidegger has often done in his etymological
reconstructions of the vocabulary of Western metaphysics – the
connections and the stratifications that echo, implicit and often
forgotten, in every particular true statement is to awaken the
memory of an indefinite network of relations (such as Wittgenstein's family resemblances, opposed to the abstract universality
of essence, genus and species) that constitute the basis of a possible
universality, namely, the persuasiveness of that statement; ideally,
for everyone.

It is a case of a universality and, first, of a critical attitude that
has been *verwunden*; taken up again in their earlier metaphysical
determination, pursued and distorted in corresponding to, that is,

in hearing, a call of Being which resonates in the epoch of the completion of metaphysics. These, too, are the transformations on account of which Heidegger, with a terminological twist that hermeneutics must always meditate afresh, believed it necessary to refer the most original essence of truth to 'freedom'.[23]

Appendix 2

The Reconstruction of Rationality

Hermeneutics has often been branded an extreme expression of the irrationalism that has permeated the greater part of continental European culture and philosophy since the first decades of the twentieth century. This accusation is launched both by the supporters of historicist rationalism (such as the followers of Lukács) and by neo-positivist scientism. And it is an accusation that is at least in part legitimate, given that the bases of hermeneutics – above all, Heideggerian ontology – are strongly polemical in relation to these two forms of rationalism, which hermeneutics considers not as opposed to one another, but rather as two moments of the same development of metaphysical reason. Recently, since both these forms of rationalism have lost their hegemonic position in our culture, the accusation of irrationalism with respect to hermeneutics has been propagated in a weaker form: it maintains that hermeneutics involves a more or less explicit rejection of argumentation, which is replaced by a kind of creative-poetic, or even purely narrative, way of philosophizing. I intend to claim here that:

1 This accusation of irrationalism is not entirely unfounded, or at least identifies a risk that is indeed present in the most well known and talked about of hermeneutic theories.
2 Hermeneutics can and must rebut this accusation by working to develop from its own original presuppositions a notion of

rationality all of its own that, without returning to the foundational procedures of traditional metaphysics, does not completely annul the specific characteristics of philosophical discourse, as distinct from, say, poetry and literature. This 'rationality of hermeneutics', or hermeneutic rationality, aims specifically to rebut the latest, weak, form taken by the accusation of irrationalism which focuses on the absence of argument in hermeneutic theory; but it can also open the way to a renewal, at least in certain respects, of the more classical historicist and scientific notions of rationality.

3 The reconstruction of a hermeneutic notion of rationality is inseparable from a reconsideration of the relation between hermeneutics and modernity.

---

1 Hermeneutic 'Irrationalism'

The present-day accusations of irrationalism laid against hermeneutics are formulated principally on the basis of a weak notion of rationality as the capacity to put forward publicly recognizable arguments rather than simple 'poetic' intuitions; this weak rationalism is often accompanied by the remains of a stronger notion of reason, that is, by the remnants of the myth of historicism and scientism. But when hermeneutics is accused of irrationalism, the reference is generally to theories such as Rorty's distinction between hermeneutics and epistemology.[1] From this point of view, a philosophical discourse that propounds publicly recognizable arguments would fall entirely within the epistemological domain (being what Kuhn calls normal science[2]), whereas what is hermeneutic is just the encounter – necessarily non-argumentative – with a new system of metaphor, or a new paradigm, whose comprehension and acceptance have nothing to do with procedures of demonstration, or at most only with persuasive argumentation. As is well known, Rorty regards his idea of hermeneutics as being well represented by Jacques Derrida – although it is not clear to what extent Rorty considers deconstruction to be an exemplary form of encounter with new systems of metaphor, or rather approaches it precisely as one of these new metaphorical languages. This problem – by no means either marginal or trifling

– may well have to do with another more radical question: is Rorty's distinction between epistemology and hermeneutics itself epistemological, that is, argumentative, or is it hermeneutic and 'poetic'? A problem like this probably seems merely formal, or even captious. But in the course of this exposition, I shall try to show that it is on the contrary crucial for the reconstruction of a hermeneutic notion of rationality. As regards Rorty, and insofar as the problem can have any meaning for him, I believe that his response to the query over his attitude towards Derrida would be that Derridian deconstruction is an exemplary way of practising philosophy as hermeneutics, namely as an encounter with and listening for new metaphorical systems; and that since this way of practising philosophy offers no justification for its own preferability, ultimately it is itself a 'poetic' and creative proposal of a new paradigm, of a new metaphorical language. However accurate Rorty's description of Derrida may be (and I believe that Derrida is not at all persuaded by it), it at least stands as a good example of what the critics call the irrationalism of hermeneutics. Hermeneutics follows Heidegger in rejecting the theory of truth as correspondence; a statement can be proved only within an opening that makes possible its verification or falsification, and the opening is something to which Dasein belongs and over which it does not have control. The project is a thrown project. The guiding metaphor for the conception of truth here is no longer grasping, 'apprehension' (com-prehension; *Begriff, con-cipere* etc.), but dwelling. To say the truth means to express – manifest, articulate – belonging to an opening in which one is always already thrown. It is not by chance that Heidegger comments so often on the verse from Hölderlin on the poetic dwelling of man: 'dichterisch wohnet der Mensch auf dieser Erde'. If the guiding metaphor for the notion of truth is dwelling, the experience of truth inevitably becomes a poetic or aesthetic experience – precisely what happens in Rorty's distinction between hermeneutics and epistemology.

At this point, hermeneutic irrationalism can also be characterized by another term – aestheticism; this seems paradoxical, if one recalls that the critique of aesthetic consciousness was one of Gadamer's key points of departure in *Truth and Method*. This paradox should serve as an indication that, if hermeneutics results in aestheticism, it is probably because it has betrayed its own originary inspiration; which, at least in Gadamer's canonical formulation, should push it in precisely the opposite direction, that is, in the direction of a defence of rationality.

My aim here will be to discuss in the briefest terms some of the forms of irrationalist – and that is, in the only sense that the word has here, non-argumentative – aestheticism that permeate much of contemporary hermeneutics. In doing so, I shall refer not only to Rorty's distinction between hermeneutics and epistemology – which is not, as one can see, just a descriptive distinction – but also to Derrida's deconstructionism. I shall leave aside the question – not irrelevant, to be sure – of whether Derrida can be considered a hermeneutic thinker: I believe that he can, at least in the sense that what he does exhibits a substantial analogy with Heidegger's *An-denken*, which has a profound deconstructive meaning as well. The difference between Derrida and the other principal hermeneutic current that has its source in Heidegger, namely, that of Gadamer, seems to me to mean only that Derrida has developed the Heideggerian legacy along lines that are distinct, but perhaps no less legitimate and certainly no less important.

Derridian deconstructionism may be characterized by the fact that, over the developmental arc of this thinking, Derrida has granted priority in both his philosophical practice and his self-interpretation to the archetype of Mallarmé's *coup de dés* over the more argumentative approach that could still be seen in the introductory chapter to *Of Grammatology*[3] ('The End of the Book and the Beginning of Writing'), where Derrida seemed to justify what we might call the grammatological turn by appealing to a kind of epochal change. The argument, as the reader will recall, ran more or less as follows: today, owing to a conjunction of circumstances that are not easily described in full, the word 'write' has taken the place previously occupied by the term 'language' [*linguaggio*], which in its turn had only recently replaced other terms such as action, movement, thought, reflection, unconscious etc. For the rest of the page, Derrida continues the description of the historical transformations that in some sense explain and, we have to believe, also justify the proposal of grammatology. This text, so far as I am aware, is a kind of *hápax legómenon* in Derrida's work; nowhere else has Derrida provided, or even set out to provide, an argued justification of his 'method' (with many scare quotes), or of the terms and ideas to which his attention periodically turns. (Might it be that he too supposes, tacitly, hermeneutico-circularly, a 'canon', a common *logos*, a kind of experience?) Not only is the beginning of the deconstructive meditation not justified by argumentation (either in general or in particular instances), when put into practice – and this is of course said without the slightest disparagement – it increasingly resembles a *performance*, the effect of which is not easily distinguished from that of an aesthetic experience; this may perhaps explain why there is ultimately no Derridian 'school', with a doctrine of its own determining the problems on which work is required etc. (Incidently, Nietzsche and his Zarathustra wanted precisely this.) Derrida, one might say, cannot be followed, but only imitated; just like artists. There is no need for me to say that in Derrida's view this is probably not regarded as a limitation, but rather as something positively desired. From the point of view that I am defending here, however, all this carries a very high risk (if such it be) of aestheticism, similar to that which I believe one finds in Rorty. In distinction from Rorty, and in common with much French philosophy of the second half of the twentieth century, this aestheticism is comprised in part by a link with literary experience, especially Mallarméan symbolism and, perhaps to a lesser extent, the twentieth-century avant-garde. The arbitrary character of the choice for deconstruction and of its specific themes seems to me to speak of a symbolist faith in the possibility of arriving at the 'essential', or at least of saying something meaningful, from any point whatsoever of the traditional text, or even of the language within which we stand. If instead one focuses not on the arbitrariness of the deconstructive choice, but on Derrida's preference for the margins – the frame, the borders etc. – then another metaphysics lies in ambush: that which looks for the true or perhaps the most authentic, the most worthy of being said and thought, in what lies outside the canon. But this attitude too, which to be sure is no more than a risk in Derrida, can nonetheless be called aestheticist, in a broad sense that encompasses the rhetoric of the *bohémien* artist, the damned poet and the creative intellectual as excluded from the harmony of the bourgeois order and so on.

Having travelled thus far, the aestheticism, and irrationalism, of hermeneutics seems to have taken on two different meanings: first, it is defined in relation to Rorty's distinction between hermeneutics and epistemology, in which the comprehension of new systems of metaphors is contrasted to normal-scientific activity that argues from within a given and accepted paradigm. This comprehension can only be a kind of aesthetic 'assimilation' of the world and to the world opened by the new system of metaphor understood as Heidegger understood the work of art in the 'Ursprung des Kunstwerkes' ('The Origin of the Work of Art'). In this sense, the assimilation, to call it such, excludes argumentation, demonstration, logical cogency. In a second sense, the deconstructionist version of hermeneutics seems to imply irrationalism inasmuch as, to escape metaphysics, it rejects all argumentative justification of its own choices and way of proceeding, presenting itself rather as a *coup de dés*. However, at least in my view, this entails the burdensome recurrence of a metaphysical – above all, symbolist – background; at which point, the anti-metaphysical vocation of hermeneutics is betrayed.

It is possible to demonstrate the connection between these two forms, or inflections or versions, of hermeneutic aestheticism and irrationalism by referring back to the critique of aesthetic consciousness developed by Gadamer in *Truth and Method*. There, as the reader will recall, aesthetic consciousness is said to consider the work of art as a closed and separate universe that one approaches via a well-honed and intuitive *Erlebnis*. In this sense, the Gadamerian critique seems to be applicable primarily to Rorty and the conception of the hermeneutic act as an encounter with a wholly new system of metaphors. But the absolute newness and autonomy of the work of art that offers itself to the well-honed taste of the aesthetic *Erlebnis* has its correlate in the creative genius – which in the post-Romantic age has come to lose the teleologico-natural roots it once had in Kant, remaining pure arbitrariness. And in this sense, the Gadamerian critique seems to strike too at the arbitrary 'genius' of the deconstructive act.

These observations are significant in my view, for what I am trying to show is that, if hermeneutics gives way to either of the forms of aestheticism and irrationalism that I have described, it will betray its own premises and return to metaphysics. And first and foremost, it will find itself re-proposing a clearly metaphysical conception of aesthetic experience.

2 The 'Foundation' of Hermeneutics

Although Gadamer's critique of aesthetic consciousness provides a good way out of hermeneutic aestheticism and irrationalism, the recurrent suspicions of traditionalism or, at the other extreme, of relativism raised by his critics are in part justified by the fact that he has never radically addressed, on the basis of his own premisses, the question of hermeneutic 'rationality'. In spite of its richness, *Truth and Method* does not put forward an explicit 'foundation' of hermeneutics to which one can appeal as proof of, or at least as a persuasive argument for, its general validity. In one respect, it is as though Gadamer professes the truth of hermeneutics in the name of a phenomenological analysis of aesthetic and historical (historiographical) experience; or, to put it another way, by showing that what really takes place in our experience of the work of art or in the encounter with texts from the past is not adequately understood or described by philosophical theories dominated by the prejudices of scientism. If this were the case, however, we would have to regard Gadamer's theory of interpretation as founded on an objective, metaphysically true and adequate, description of what hermeneutical experience is really of – which would be an obvious contradiction, given the polemic directed in *Truth and Method* against every pretence of science and philosophy to provide an 'objective' description of reality.

Alongside, or at a deeper level than, this phenomenological analysis of hermeneutic experience, there is in *Truth and Method* also a historical reconstruction of the process by which the methodological self-consciousness of the modern *Geisteswissenschaften* developed in the direction of a general philosophy of existence conceived as interpretation, that is, in the direction of a hermeneutic ontology. What remains unclear throughout the book is the relation between these two levels of argumentation – the phenomenologico-analytic and the historico-reconstructive. Gadamer shows that the predominance of scientific methodologism beginning in the seventeenth century obscured significant elements of the preceding traditional philosophy, along with all the social, practical and aesthetic implications of notions such as *sensus communis*, discretion, taste, culture etc. The reasons for speaking of obscuration, of loss (even if these are not precisely the terms he uses) seem to lie in a phenomenological analysis of experience; this cannot, however, be understood as a more adequate description of what really happens, at least not if Gadamer wishes to avoid self-contradiction. If this is how things stand, perhaps Rorty is right: the only way to 'adopt' a hermeneutic point of view in philosophy may well be to approach it as though it were a work of art, or a discursive universe that is to be intuitively assimilated (although precisely *why* is a problem that must ultimately be posed to aesthetic experience as well), in much the same way as an anthropologist assimilates (or is assimilated to) the other culture that he or she wishes to study 'from within'. But this way of adopting or assimilating the philosophical position of hermeneutics would contradict another central point in Gadamer's theory, namely, his critique of aesthetic consciousness and aesthetic *Erlebnis*. For the same reasons, I believe that we cannot expect Gadamer to recommend the adoption of hermeneutics as a *coup de dés*, which in the deconstructionist perspective seems to be legitimated by its arbitrariness alone. From Gadamer's point of view, this would look like an unjustifiable revival of the late and post-romantic vision of the artist as an uprooted, marginalized genius excluded from bourgeois social rationality.

The solution to this problem – how to avoid the irrationalism that seems to be implicit in the very 'foundation' of hermeneutics – may be possible by way of an attempted radicalization of *Truth and Method* with a view to clarifying the reconstruction of the development of the methodological self-consciousness of the *Geisteswissenschaften*. The direction of this radicalization is indicated by Gadamer himself precisely inasmuch as the phenomenological analysis of experience is never separated from the historical reference to the tradition: thus, for example, when he speaks of the *applicatio* as a model of hermeneutic understanding, the discussion is founded on Aristotle and the tradition of juridical hermeneutics; the same goes for the crucially important pages in which the analysis and the critique of aesthetic consciousness is conducted in continuous dialogue with Kant, Kierkegaard and twentieth-century aesthetics. All this, radically – and perhaps beyond the explicit intentions of Gadamer himself – means that there is no 'phenomenological' analysis of experience (the inverted commas cannot be avoided here) that is not conditioned, that is, made possible and qualified, by the fact of belonging to a tradition. Even the *coup de dés* is described in reference to the historical experience of an artist from the past. Its arbitrariness, consequently, can only reside in the refusal to explain why precisely this term and this specific historical reference are chosen. But is this not a situation familiar to hermeneutics – that one who is dominated by prejudices cannot recognize and thematize them as such? Is there not here something that Gadamer would call a forgetting [*oblio*] or a remotion of *Wirkungsgeschichte*? In the very principle of *Wirkungsgeschichte*,[4] in the opposition of *wirkungsgeschichtliches Bewusstsein* to aesthetic consciousness and Enlightenment historiography – that is, in the thesis that a work of art, a text or a trace of the past can only be understood on the basis of the history of its effects, of the interpretations by way of which it has been handed down to us – there may lie a clue for the reconstruction of an idea of hermeneutic rationality. The fact that Gadamer does not fully clarify the relation between the 'phenomenological' and historical aspects of his discourse may well be due to the fact that he does not adequately apply to his own theory the principles that the theory itself wishes to uphold. To radicalize the premisses set down in *Truth and Method*, therefore, means to recognize that hermeneutics as theory can only be coherently legitimized by demonstrating that it is in its turn nothing more than a correct hermeneutic interpretation of a message from the past, or in any case from 'somewhere else' to which, in some degree, it itself always already belongs – since this belonging is the very condition for the possibility of receiving messages. The critique of objectivism and postivistic scientism would be neither radical nor coherent if hermeneutics did not aim to stand as a more adequate description of what experience, existence, Dasein, really is. 'There are no facts, only interpretations,' wrote Nietzsche;[5] but this too is not a statement of fact, but 'only' an interpretation.

In a somewhat paradoxical fashion, it is only the radical awareness of itself as interpretative, and neither descriptive nor objective, that guarantees hermeneutics the possibility of arguing rationally on its own behalf. The 'reasons' offered by hermeneutics in order to demonstrate its own theoretical validity amount to an interpretative reconstruction of the history of modern philosophy, broadly similar to the reasons put forward by Nietzsche to affirm that 'God is dead'. This affirmation too was not, and did not wish to be, a descriptive metaphysical statement on the non-existence of God; it was a narrative interpretation of the history of our culture, aiming to show that it is no longer necessary, nor 'morally' possible, to believe in God – at least not in the God of the onto-theological tradition. In effect, this amounts to a 'logical' (that is common-sense) expectation that someone who has read Marx, Nietzsche, Freud and Wittgenstein etc. can 'no longer' accept certain ideas, beliefs or assume certain practical or theoretical attitudes. As we might say, 'After Marx, after Nietzsche, after — how can one still believe that —?' This 'after' is not a logically cogent 'given that', a strong foundation; but neither is it purely and simply an invitation to share in a certain taste – all of which takes us back to the aestheticist horizon of hermeneutic irrationalism. The very idea that, if not a proof or a logical foundation, this 'after' must be a merely aesthetic *Erlebnis* clearly betrays its own dependence on scientism. In a certain sense, it is true that the 'model' of the hermeneutic notion of truth and of the experience of truth is an aesthetic model; but – as Gadamer has shown in the first part of *Truth and Method* – not in the sense of 'aesthetic' that came to prevail after Kant, and that echoes, for example, through the Kierkegaardian idea of aesthetic existence.

---

3 Hermeneutics and Modernity

As I said at the beginning, the reconstruction of rationality from a hermeneutic perspective calls first and foremost for a radicalization of the philosophical premises on which the development of hermeneutics rests. That it is only a matter of radicalization signifies moreover that the form of argumentation I have tried to describe by recalling the example of Nietzsche's dictum 'God is dead' is to a considerable extent already present in today's hermeneutic activity; not only in Gadamer, but also in Rorty and, far more clearly, in Derrida. The 'psychoanalytic', or psychotherapeutic, deconstruction of Western metaphysics that Rorty conducts in *Philosophy and the Mirror of Nature*, the multiple deconstructive activity of Derrida and, naturally, Gadamer's 'historical preparation' in *Truth and Method* are the obvious examples of this kind of narrative-interpretative argumentation. Yet to escape the risks of relativism, aestheticism and irrationalism altogether, it seems to me indispensable that the ontological implications of hermeneutic discourse be made explicit.

Hermeneutics, as a philosophical theory, 'proves' its own validity only by appealing to a historical process of which it proposes a reconstruction that shows how 'choosing' hermeneutics – as opposed to positivism, for example – is preferable or more justified. This formulation might sound too hard or rigid to many hermeneutic philosophers, but it seems indispensable to me as a first step towards the reconstruction of hermeneutic rationality. As I have said, I do not believe that interpretative reconstructions of the history of modern philosophy such as Gadamer provides in his work, or one finds in Nietzsche's writings, or that is Rorty's in *Philosophy and the Mirror of Nature*, or which, albeit in a deliberately fragmentary and partial way, is presented by many of Derrida's texts, are reducible to 'poetic' images. It is not by chance, in this respect, that the problematic within which hermeneutics was born and has developed up until the present day is that of the validity of the *Geisteswissenschaften*, and of their distinction from purely poetic representations of other cultural universes and of forms of life from the past. There is no question here of a vicious circle that could undermine the very claims to validity of hermeneutics. The truth is rather that hermeneutics can defend its theoretical validity only to the precise degree that the interpretative reconstruction of history is a rational activity – in which, that is, one can argue, and not only intuit, *fühlen, Einfühlen* etc.

Ontology – in the specific sense that the term has here, and that I shall explain in a moment – has to do with all this because without it hermeneutics risks appearing as no more than a theory of the multiplicity (irreducible and inexplicable, to be accepted as one accepts life itself, or as an 'ultimate' quasi-metaphysical fact) of conceptual schemes; where it too is only one conceptual scheme amongst others, to be preferred solely on the basis of a choice that cannot be reasoned, and which may take the form either of an aesthetic encounter with a new system of metaphors, as in Rorty, or of Derrida's avant-garde-symbolist *coup de dés*. Only if the birth and development of hermeneutics is not simply a question of conceptual schemes (that do not, as such, touch the Being-real 'out there'), but belongs to what Heidegger calls the destiny of Being, can the theoretical choice in favour of hermeneutics, and also specific interpretative choices (like the Derridian deconstructions), be anything more than aesthetic *Erlebnisse* or acrobatic *coup de dés*.

Schematically speaking, what comes to be called the irrationalism of hermeneutics is the aestheticism that one can discover in authors such as Rorty and Derrida, and which constitutes a risk in Gadamer too, at least insofar as he does not clarify the way in which hermeneutics 'proves' its own validity as a theory. A clarification of this kind calls for hermeneutics to cease thinking of itself, more or less consciously and explicitly, as a theory founded on a phenomenological analysis that is 'adequate' to experience. Hermeneutics is itself 'only interpretation'. Its own claims to validity are not founded on a presumption of access to the things themselves; to be consistent with the Heideggerian critique of the idea of truth as correspondence from which it professes to draw its inspiration, it can only conceive of itself as the response to a message, or as the interpretative articulation of its own belonging to a tra-dition [*tra-dizione*], *Über-lieferung*. This tradition is not simply a succession of 'conceptual schemes' – for thought in this way, it would still leave an *ontos on* outside itself, a thing in itself thought in metaphysical terms. If it wishes to escape this relapse into metaphysics, hermeneutics must make explicit its own ontological backgound, that is, the Heideggerian idea of a destiny of Being that is articulated as the concatenation of openings, of the systems of metaphors that make possible and qualify our experience of the world. Hermeneutics conceives of itself as a moment within this destiny; and it argues for its own validity by proposing a reconstruction of the destiny-tradition from which it arises. This reconstruction is itself obviously an interpretation; but not 'only' an interpretation in the sense in which such an expression still implies the idea that beyond it there may be an *ontos on* that remains external to our conceptual schemes. The destiny of Being, naturally, is given only in an interpretation, and does not have objective-deterministic cogency: it is *Ge-Schick* in the sense of a *Schickung*, a sending. We can translate thus: the rationality we have reached consists in the fact that, essentially involved in a process (into which we are always-already 'thrown') we always-already know, at least to a certain extent, where we are going and how we must go there. But to orient ourselves, we need to reconstruct and interpret the process in as complete and persuasive a manner as possible. It would be an error to believe that we can jump outside the process, somehow grasping the *arche*, the principle, the essence or the ultimate structure. Rationality is simply the guiding thread that can be comprehended by listening attentively to the messages of the *Schickung*. Both the theoretical choice for hermeneutics and the specific choices of our interpretative activity can be justified by argumentation on this basis.

The ontological radicalization of hermeneutics put forward here has significant consequences, or at the very least makes a difference. One of these consequences concerns the relation of hermeneutics to modernity – or, in other terms, to modern thought as a thought of the advent of nihilism. If hermeneutics has no source of validity beyond its belonging to an *Über-lieferung* which is specifically that of modern thought, its relation with this tradition will have to be thought in different and far more positive terms than those which characterize, for example, Gadamer's position in *Truth and Method*. The relation of hermeneutics to modern scientism or to the world of technical rationality cannot be simply, or even primarily, that of a polemical rejection – as if it were a matter, yet again, of opposing a truer knowledge and a vision of more authentic existence to the theoretical and practical vagaries of modernity. Rather, it is a matter of recognizing and demonstrating that hermeneutics is a 'consequence' of modernity and a confutation of it.

For hermeneutics this entails the task of developing an important and controversial aspect of its inheritance from Heidegger; and that is, his conception of the *Ge-Stell*, of the technical-scientific world, understood both as the accomplishment of metaphysics and as the first announcement of its overcoming (as in the

famous passage from *Identity and Difference* on the 'first oppressing flash of *Ereignis*'). Hermeneutics is not a theory that opposes
an authenticity of existence founded on the privilege of the human
sciences to the alienation of the rationalized society; it is rather a
theory that tries to grasp the meaning of the transformation (of
the idea) of Being that has been produced as a consequence of the
techno-scientific rationalization of our world. It is not hard to see
that this way of developing the hermeneutic discourse is different
to that which, with aesthetical implications, characterizes writers
such as Rorty and Derrida. It may perhaps be closer to Foucault
and to what he once called the 'ontology of actuality'.

As a theory of modernity – in the objective and subjective senses
of the genitive – hermeneutics could also recover, at least in part,
the two principal senses that rationality has had in the modern
tradition: that is, the senses linked to the positive sciences and to
historicism respectively. As for the sciences, they could come to
be no longer considered just as ways to push the metaphysical
oblivion of Being to its extreme, but also as conditions, along with
technology, for a transformation in the meaning of Being in the
direction of its post-metaphysical givenness. The world of scientific 'objectification' – as Heidegger demonstrates in the concluding pages of the essay 'The Age of the World Picture' – is also that
in which, by a kind of inflative process (the images proliferate and
so undermine any pretensions to objectivity), the metaphysical
qualification, or *Wesen*, of Being tends to dissolve. As for historicist rationality, it is all too clear that the way of arguing for the
validity of hermeneutics has a great deal to do with historicism.
In contrast to the metaphysical historicism of the nineteenth
century (Hegel, Comte, Marx), hermeneutics does not take the
meaning of history to be a 'fact' that must be recognized,
cultivated and accepted (again as a kind of metaphysical finality);
the guiding thread of history appears, is given, only in an act of
interpretation that is confirmed in dialogue with other possible
interpretations and that, in the final analysis, leads to a modification of the actual situation in a way that makes the interpretation
'true'. For this reason, I repeat, the interpretative reconstruction
of history that hermeneutics proposes is not simply a new poetic
vocabulary that offers itself to an aesthetic *Erlebnis*: and anyway,
how could a philosophical system that claimed to be universally

true, such as the Hegelian system, be approached as though it were a poetic creation? Would this not be a way of misunderstanding precisely that which it believes to be most essential to itself? The novelty and the importance of hermeneutics ultimately consists in the affirmation that the rational (argumentative) interpretation of history is not 'scientific' in the positivistic sense and yet neither is it purely 'aesthetic'. The task of contemporary hermeneutics seems to be that of articulating in an ever more complete and explicit form this original inspiration; which means furthermore the task of corresponding responsibly to the appeal arising from its inheritance.

Notes

~~~~~~~~

Chapter 1 The Nihilistic Vocation of Hermeneutics

1 Cf. my essay 'Ermeneutica nuova koiné' now in the volume *Etica dell'interpretazione* (Rosenberg & Dellier, Turin, 1989), pp. 38–48.
2 On this, cf. L. Pareyson, *Estetica. Teoria della formatività* (Bompiani, Milan, 1954), pp. 75ff.
3 H.-G. Gadamer, *Truth and Method* [1960] (Sheed & Ward, London, 1979).
4 In spite of the best intentions of the author, this is the direction taken by V. Mathieu's 'Manifesto di un movimento ermeneutico universale', *Filosofia*, 43 (May–August 1992), 2.
5 I am of course thinking of the 'paradigms' spoken of by Thomas Kuhn in *The Structure of Scientific Revolutions* [1962] (University of Chicago Press, Chicago, 1970).
6 This because – by virtue of the temporality of consciousness that keeps Cassirer no less than Heidegger from thinking Being as simple presence – it is difficult to distinguish the activity of symbolization (which would be the translation in Cassirer's language of the term interpretation) from the concrete forms that it takes in history, from the languages that it inherits, in short, from its finitude; which, rather contradictorily on the basis of the same Cassirerean presuppositions, is ultimately frustrated by a characteristically Hegelian teleological structure of taste, where historicity is at once recognized and removed. On this, cf. the introduction by L. Lugarini to the Italian translation of Cassirer's 'Essay on Man' of 1923, 'Saggio sull'uomo', trans E. Arnaud (La Nuova Italia, Florence, 1987), p. 17.
7 Cf. E. Cassirer, *The Philosophy of Symbolic Forms,* Vol 1: *Language* [1923], trans. R. Mannheim (Yale University Press, New Haven, 1955), p. 83.
8 Cf. e.g. aphorism 22 in *Beyond Good and Evil* [1886] (Penguin Books, Harmondsworth, 1979).
9 Cf. J. Habermas, *The Philosophical Discourse of Modernity*, trans. F. Lawrence (Polity Press, Cambridge, 1985), ch. 3, pt. 1 n .4, p. 392.

10 Cf. 'The Reconstruction of Rationality', published here as appendix 2.
11 Cf. above all my essay 'Heideggers Nihilismus: Nietzsche als Interpret Heideggers', in F. von Hermann and W. Biemel (eds), *Kunst und Technik. Gedächtnisschrift zum 100. Geburtstag von Martin Heidegger* (Klostermann, Frankfurt a.M., 1989).

Chapter 2 Science

1 M. Heidegger, 'The Origin of the Work of Art', in *Holzwege* (Vittorio Klostermann, Frankfurt a.M., 1977), p. 62.
2 M. Heidegger, *What is Called Thinking?* [1954], trans. J. Glenn Gray (Harper & Row, New York, 1968), p. 33.
3 R. Rorty, *Philosophy and the Mirror of Nature* (Blackwell, Oxford, 1980), ch. 7.
4 Cf. the various essays collected in R. Rorty, *Contingency, Irony and Solidarity* [1989] (Cambridge University Press, 1992).
5 Many important analogies between Popper and not insignificant aspects of hermeneutics are illustrated clearly in D. Antiseri's fine work *Le ragioni del pensiero debole* (Armando, Rome, 1992); on metaphysics and its meaning in Popper's fallibilism, cf. esp. pp. 64ff.
6 K. O. Apel has paid particular attention to the 'hermeneutic' aspects of Peirce's thought and to the meaning of the notion of an 'experimental community of researchers': cf. *Transformation der Philosophie* (Suhrkamp, Frankfurt a.M., 1973).
7 In *The Structure of Scientific Revolutions*, cited above, Thomas Kuhn advanced the now well-known thesis that the experimental sciences do not develop in a linear fashion, resolving the problems left open by earlier research. Such linearity occurs, but only within the bounds of a single paradigm, that is, within the horizon of a certain language, a certain method, a certain criterion for distinguishing between what is relevant and what is not. The paradigms change historically, but not because they come to be seen as false in the light of some more general criterion. Rather, when they go into crisis because they fail to resolve certain problems, and when another alternative paradigm presents itself, they are simply abandoned by the scientific community; and this is what Kuhn calls a 'scientific revolution'.
8 Cf. G. Vattimo, 'Ermeneutica e teoria dell'agire comunicativo', in L. Sciola and L. Ricolfi (eds), *Il soggetto dell'azione* (Franco Angeli, Milan, 1989).
9 Cf. above all § 6 of E. Husserl, *Crisis in the European Sciences and Transcendental Phenomenology* [1954] (Northwestern University Press, Evanston, Ill., 1970).
10 Cf. on the other hand books (mostly of Anglo-Saxon origin) such as J. Bleicher, *Contemporary Hermeneutics* (Routledge, London, 1980), that include Apel and Habermas as fully fledged exponents of 'critical hermeneutics'.
11 H.-G. Gadamer, *Reason in the Age of Science* [1976], trans. F. Lawrence (MIT, Cambridge, Mass, 1981).
12 K. Mannheim, *Ideology and Utopia* [1929] (Routledge & Kegan Paul, London, 1968).

13 E. Bloch, *Gesamtausgabe, vd. 16: Geist der Utopie* [1923] (Suhrkamp, Frankfurt a.M., 1971).

14 It seems to me that a similar existentialist 'tone' may be heard in Gadamer; and in many pages of Derrida's essay on Levinas ('Violence and Metaphysics', trans. A. Bass (Routledge & Kegan Paul, London, 1981)), on which, see my essay 'Metafisica, violenza, secolarizzazione' in G. Vattimo (ed.) *Filosofia '86* (Laterza, Rome-Bari, 1987), pp. 71–94.

15 Cf. M. Heidegger, *Identity and Difference*, trans. J. Stambaugh [1957] (Harper & Row, New York, 1969), p. 38. The *Ge-Stell*, which I have suggested be translated into Italian as '*im-posizione*' [im-position] (cf. my trans. of Heidegger, *Saggi e discorsi* (Mursia, Milan, 1976) p. 14) indicates the ensemble (*Ge-*) of the *Stellen* (the position, the disposition etc. that constitutes the essence of modern technology); and it is precisely in this ensemble, which is also the high point and triumph of metaphysics, i.e. of the presentation and veiling of Being in the subject–object relation, that Heidegger sees the first glimmer of a possible overcoming of metaphysics itself. I have commented on this aspect of Heidegger's thought in various essays; cf. e.g. the final essay in *The End of Modernity* (Polity Press, Cambridge, 1988).

16 This is a text from 1938, included in M. Heidegger, *The Question Concerning Technology*, trans. W. Lovitt (Harper & Row, New York, 1977), pp. 115–54.

17 Ibid., p. 129 n. 6.

18 Ibid., p. 135.

19 Ibid., p. 135 n. 13.

20 Ibid., p. 136. [Vattimo modifies the existing Italian translation (Chiodi) by translating '*verweigert*' as '*preclusa*' rather than '*vietata*'. This suggests 'closed off' rather than 'forbidden'. – Trans.]

21 Cf. e.g. *Crisis*, cited above, § 34 d.

Chapter 3 Ethics

1 F. Nietzsche, *The Will to Power*, trans. W. Kaufmann and R. J. Hollingdale (Random House, New York, 1968), p. 38.

2 It is curious – but perhaps not too strange if one follows Heidegger in thinking that the tradition of philosophy up until Nietzsche has been under the constant domination of the metaphysics of presence – that if one looks in the philosophical tradition for a definition of violence, one ends up having to go back to an essentialist definition (or, which is a slight variation, one drawn from natural law). Violence is what prevents a being from realizing its own natural potential: which in the end is not very different from the Aristotelian doctrine of 'natural places' (the stone tends to go downward, fire upward etc.), on the basis of which one defines that which is *katà* and *parà physin*, according to or against (or beyond) nature. Important ideas pointing in the 'hermeneutic' direction that I am trying to follow may be found, however, in P. Ricoeur, *Violence et langage* [1967], now in *Lectures I. Autour du politique* (Seuil, Paris, 1991), pp. 131–41.

3 Cf. F. Nietzsche, *Human All Too Human* [1879] (Cambridge University Press, Cambridge, 1986) and *Nietzsches Werke: Kritische Gesamtausgabe,*

ed. G. Colli and M. Montinari, vol. 4, pp. 437, 431: 'Bei einem weniger gewaltsam Charakter des sozialen Lebens verlieren die letzten Entscheidungen (über sogenannte ewige Fragen) ihre Wichtigkeit. Man bedenke, wie selten schon jetzt ein Mensch etwas mit ihnen zu thun hat': 'Where the character of social life is *less violent*, the ultimate decisions (on the so-called eternal questions) lose their importance. One reflects how seldom man has anything to do with them today' (Fragment 40.7). 'Metaphysik und Philosophie sind Versuch, sich gewaltsam der fruchtbarsten Gebiete zu bemächtigen': 'Metaphysics and philosophy are attempts to gain control over the most fertile territories *by force*' (Fragment 40.21). [Both of these passages have been translated by the present translator, following the Italian edition quoted by Vattimo. The emphasis in each case is Vattimo's.]

4 [The Italian runs: '*l'esperienza della verità è condizionata dal fatto di disporre di, e di essere disposti in, un linguaggio.*' My translation here does not capture the exact play on the verb '*disporre*', which can mean both 'to use or have at one's disposal' and (in its passive form) 'to be set out or to be articulated'. – Trans.]

5 Cf. e.g. Apel, *Transformation der Philosophie*, see ch. 2 n. 6 above.

6 Cf. ibid., the final essay on 'Das Apriori der Kommunikationgemeinschaft und die Grundlagen der Ethik'. On Apel and ethics cf. also R. Mancini's study *Linguaggio ed etica. La semiotica transcendentale di Karl-Otto Apel* (Marietti, Genoa, 1988).

7 Cf. e.g. the conclusion to the first part of Gadamer, *Truth and Method* (see ch. 1 n. 3), pp. 146ff.

8 It may be that Rorty's theory was constructed in direct polemic against it. Cf. e.g. Rorty, *Philosophy and the Mirror of Nature*, pp. 379ff. Regarding redescriptions, cf. *Contingency, Irony and Solidarity* cited above, ch. 2 n. 3.

9 The idea of redescription is for the most part used by Rorty only in contexts that have to do with the constitution of philosophy, of poetry etc. When it is a matter of morals, his preferred concept is that of solidarity, as is the case in *Contingency, Irony and Solidarity*. Nonetheless, as he writes in the final essay of this book ('Solidarity'), the ironic liberal (the redescriber who is self-aware etc. is 'someone for whom this sense was a matter of imaginative identification with the details of others' lives, rather than a recognition of something antecedently shared', p. 190. It is not far-fetched, then, to see a relation between redescriptions and solidarity: the latter, since it cannot found itself on a metaphysical kind of universalism, depends on 'which similarities and dissimilarities strike us as salient, and that such salience is a function of a historically contingent final vocabulary', p. 192. Such a final vocabulary certainly has something to do with redescriptions (it conditions them, is modified by them, and so on). My impression is that Rorty does not develop his reflections on these connections far enough.

10 Cf. G. Deleuze, *Foucault* [1986], trans. S. Hand (Athlone Press, London, 1988), p. 106.

11 Cf. P. Klossowski, *Nietzsche et le circle vicieux* [1969] (Mercure de France, Paris, 1969).

12 Of course, it would be very simplistic to reduce Rorty's redescriptions, or Klossowski's conspiracy and Foucault's variations in lifestyle, to a purely aesthetic denominator. One can hear echoes of the existentialist tradition of authenticity as the sole possible ethical imperative in the age of nihilism,

and also, from a more recent time, the same broadly 'ecological' concern as manifests itself in efforts to save animal or vegetable species on the way to extinction. At the root of these efforts lies the idea that the survival of the human species has in the past been assured by the multiplicity of cultures, that is, of responses that it has known how to make to the challenges of the environment. The preservation of this multiplicity for the future seems to be an indispensable condition of survival. On the significance of the conspiracy in Klossowski, and on the relations that could be established between Rorty and Foucault, cf. my essay 'Il paradigma e l'arcano' in G. Vattimo and M. Ferraris (eds), *Filosofia '93* (Laterza, Rome-Bari, 1994), pp. 231–50.

13 Cf. e.g. ch. 5 of *Contingency, Irony and Solidarity*, esp. pp. 117–18.

14 One is reminded again of the idea of a 'forming form' theorized by Pareyson in his *Estetica*.

15 Cf. § 3 of the final chapter of Rorty, *Philosophy and the Mirror of Nature,* pp. 373–9.

16 On the whole of this orientation, profoundly related to the spread of hermeneutics, cf. F. Volpi, 'Tra Aristotele e Kant: orizzonti, prospettive e limiti del dibattito sulla riabilitazione della filosofia pratica', in C. A. Viano (ed.), *Teorie etiche contemporanee* (Bollati Boringhieri, Turin, 1990), pp. 128–48.

17 Cf. the essay 'The Truth of Hermeneutics', appendix 1 to this book.

18 But why does hermeneutic ethics have to be an ethics of continuity? One might suspect that, once again, it is a case here of a return to the classical ideal of harmony: the good as the beauty of an achieved conciliation, as a non-conflictual belonging to a totality. But, to speak of an open continuity always established afresh on the basis of a risky interpretation, as opposed to the idea of a kind of Hegelian absolute subject, shows that what we are facing here is a *Verwindung* of metaphysics, i.e. according to the sense that the term has in Heidegger, a 'distorted and transformed' resumption of the need for foundations that guided metaphysics, and that one cannot simply lay aside like a piece of discarded clothing or an error that has been recognized as such (for this would be to claim that one had finally arrived at the objective truth, thereby repeating the metaphysical error). Cf. also ch. 4 n. 14 below. Continuity seems to be the only meaning of rationality in the epoch of nihilism (and cf. 'The Reconstruction of Rationality', appendix 2 to this book). For metaphysics it was a case of establishing itself on the ultimate and certain basis of primary foundations; for nihilistic hermeneutics it is a case of arguing in such a way that each new interpretation enters into dialogue with those that came before and does not constitute an incomprehensible dia-'logical' leap. In the end (see the conclusion to this chapter) the imperative of continuity belongs to a rationality that does not define itself in relation to objective structures that thinking should and could reflect, but to respect and to *pietas* for the neighbour. For this reason too, however, continuity cannot be defined abstractly, but must refer to a determinate neighbour or neighbours.

19 On the history and meaning of the term, and on its use above all in Davidson, see the eighth study by D. Sparti, *Sopprimere la lontananza uccide. D. Davidson e la teoria dell'interpretazione* (La Nuova Italia, Florence, 1994), pp. 54ff.

Chapter 4 Religion

1 Cf. W. Dilthey, *Gesammelte Schriften* (Teubner, Leipzig-Berlin, 1914), vol. 5: *Die geistige Welt*, pp. 317–18.

2 On this point, see the Introduction to my *Schleiermacher filosofo dell'interpretazione* [1967] (Mursia, Milan, 1985), and the bibliography given therein. Regarding the observations that follow, see also of course M. Ferraris, *Storia dell'ermeneutica* (Bompiani, Milan, 1988).

3 Gadamer, *Truth and Method*, pp. 192–235.

4 I am thinking primarily of certain texts by M. Cacciari, such as *L'angelo necessario* (Adelphi, Milan, 1886); and *Dell'inizio* (Adelphi, Milan, 1990).

5 See, in addition to the most important of J. Hillman's writings, such as *The Myth of Analysis* [1972] (Northwestern University Press, Evanston, Ill., 1972) and *Re-vision of Psychology* [1975]; also J. Hillman and D. L. Miller, *The New Polytheism: The Rebirth of the Gods and Goddesses* (New York, 1974). Cf. also various chapters in the *Trattato di psicologia analitica*, ed. A. Carotenuto (Utet, Turin, 1992).

6 See esp. the 1978 essay by Odo Marquard, 'Lob des Polytheismus (In Praise of Polytheism)', in *A Farewell to Matters of Principle* (Oxford University Press, New York, 1989).

7 Aristotle's expression may be found in *Metaphysics* IV. 2. 1003a33. The phrase from St Paul ('Multifariam, multisque, modis olim loquens, Deus patribus in prophetis: novissime diebus istis locutus est nobis in Filio') is in Hebrews 1: 1–2.

8 Joachim's mystical doctrine is entirely unique and, perhaps for this reason, has left traces in almost all subsequent history of European thought: on this, see H. de Lubac, *La postérité spirituelle de Joachim de Fiore*, 2 vols [1979–81] (Dessain et Tobra, Paris, 1972/82). See also Joachim, *Enchiridion super Apocalypsim*, ed. E. K. Burger (Toronto, 1986), and with a Latin text and Italian translation by A. Tagliapietra (Feltrinelli, Milan, 1994).

9 F. D. E. Schleiermacher, *On Religion: Speeches to its Cultured Despisers* [1799], trans. J. Oman (Harper & Row, New York, 1958), p. 91 (the second discourse).

10 Novalis, *Die Christheit oder Europa* [1799, but publ. in 1826] in *Dichter über ihre Dichtungen*, vol. 15, ed. H.-J. Mähl (Heimeran, 1976), pp. 60–8.

11 I am referring here above all to texts such as R. Girard, *Violence and the Sacred* [1972], trans. P. Gregory (Athlone Press, London, 1988) and *Things Hidden Since the Foundation of the World* [1978], trans. P. Gregory (Athlone Press, London, 1987).

12 H. Blumenberg, *The Legitimacy of the Modern Age* [1966], trans. R. M. Wallace (MIT, Cambridge, Mass., 1983).

13 The work of revealing the 'human all too human' background of all moral and metaphysical systems, in short of all eternal truths, concludes in Nietzsche with the dissolution of the value of truth itself: on this, cf. my *Il soggetto e la maschera. Nietzsche e il problema della liberazione* [1974] (Bompiani, Milan, 1994), pp. 71ff.

14 This is the term that Heidegger uses to indicate the relation that, in his view, thinking maintains with metaphysics, understood as the oblivion of Being; which would therefore be 'overcome' (*überwunden*). But since it is not a case

of correcting the error of metaphysics with a more objectively true vision of how things stand, the way out of metaphysics is shown to be more complicated. We do not have before us an objectivity that, once discovered in what really is, could provide a criterion by which to change our thought; as though metaphysics might be set aside as an error or a discarded and worn-out piece of clothing. The only thing that we can do to 'get out' of the metaphysical oblivion of Being is to undertake a *Verwindung*. This term, preserving also a literal connection with *überwinden*, to overcome, means, however, in practice: to recover from an illness while still bearing its traces, to resign oneself to something. On all of this see, M. Heidegger, *The End of Philosophy* (Harper & Row, New York, 1973), pp. 85ff; and the final chapter of my *The End of Modernity*.

15 [Vattimo translates *Verwindung* by prefixing the Italian *torsione* with *dis-* to give *dis-torsione*, thereby capturing the sense of 'twisting-free' intended by Heidegger. However, in English, the word 'torsion' that conveys the sense of 'twist' is not directly transposed into 'distortion', thereby making it impossible to preserve Vattimo's wordplay precisely. – Trans.]

16 I am referring here and in what follows to Pareyson's final period of work, beginning with his major essay 'Filosofia ed esperienza religiosa' which appeared in the *Annuario filosofico* of 1985 (Mursia, Milan, 1986), pp. 7–52, and which has now been republished in *Ontologia della libertà* (Einaudi, Turin, 1995). Rereading it today, I realize that Pareyson does not accord Jesus Christ the central position – for the 'foundation' of myth and of symbol – that it seems to me his premisses quite reasonably allow. But perhaps this is why he does not carry the process of secularization as far as I believe that he could and indeed should have done. From the point of view of the thesis that I am putting forward here, all this would suggest that in Pareyson, the God of the Old Testament still holds sway. Pareyson speaks more explicitly of Christianity in the essay 'La filosofia e il problema del male,' which came out in the following year's edition of the *Annuario*, but in terms that do not seem relevant to the specific question of the relation of Jesus Christ to 'other' myths. On all of this, cf. the somewhat abbreviated analysis that I gave in the chapter 'Ermeneutica e secolarizzazione' in my *Etica dell'interpretazione*, pp. 49–62.

17 Cf. Pareyson, 'Filosofia ed esperienza religiosa', pp. 19–27.

Chapter 5 Art

1 On all these themes, cf. 'The Work of Art in the Age of Mechanical Reproduction', in W. Benjamin, *Illuminations*, trans. H. Zohn, ed. H. Arendt [1936] (Cape, London, 1982), esp. § 15.

2 I have discussed all this more fully in the first chapter of *Poesia e ontologia* [1967] (Mursia, Milano, 1985). In spite of their age, those pages still provide the theoretical background to the (relatively different) ideas that I am presenting here.

3 On the subjectivization of aesthetics that develops on the basis of Kantian critique, but *after* Kant, cf. Gadamer, *Truth and Method*, pp. 51ff.

4 Regarding the meaning and significance of the reference to the experience of art for his conception of truth, see the essay 'The Truth of Hermeneutics', appendix 1 to this book.

5 Nowadays it is thought to be the work of Schelling, formulated, with the help of his two friends, in 1795; the edition that has come down to us is from Hegel's hand and dates from 1796. There are several English translations, but the version cited here is published in F. Hölderlin, *Essays and Letters on Theory*, ed. and trans. T. Pfau (SUNY, Albany, 1988), pp. 154–6.

6 G. Lukács, *Aesthetics*, Vol 2, (Luchterland, Berlin, 1963), p. 273. The privileged position of painting is a consequence of the fact that in the medieval period art was entrusted by the church with the task of passing on the contents of the Bible to the illiterate.

7 Ibid., p. 776 .

8 Ibid., p. 778.

9 Ibid., p. 690.

10 The question of secularization, understood here as the necessity for aesthetics explicitly to take note of art's relation to its religious origins, is an outstanding example of that way of consciously placing oneself in the 'hermeneutic circle', which is, according to Heidegger, the only way to prevent the circle being logically vicious. It is also worth remembering the 'rehabilitation' of prejudice proposed by Gadamer in *Truth and Method*, pp. 241ff, which has the same sense. However, given the way our discourse is going, can we be satisfied with the thought that the question of secularization may be just a case, albeit outstanding, of the problem of the vicious circle? Will it not rather be its most radical and 'proper' meaning? Aside from anything else, thought in this way, the 'right' placement in the hermeneutic circle and the rehabilitation of prejudice (as the condition that one must be aware of in order not to be dominated by it), no longer looks like a simplistic application of psychoanalysis to philosophy. (It might otherwise seem to be so, in that the unconscious ceases to produce neurotic symptoms once it has been brought to consciousness. But not even the most orthodox of psychoanalysts believe this any more, even if they ever did.)

11 Cf. the first chapter of my *Poesia e ontologia* (n. 2 above).

12 E. Bloch, *Geist der Utopie* [1923] in *Gesamtausgabe*, vol. 2 (Suhrkamp, Frankfurt a.M., 1971) and *Das Prinzip Hoffnung* (Suhrkamp, Frankfurt a.M., 1959).

13 M. Dufrenne, *The Phenomenology of Aesthetic Experience* [1953], trans. E. Casey (Northwestern Press, Evanston, Ill., 1973).

14 Of Dilthey, cf. not only *Das Erlebnis und die Dichtung* [1906] (Vandenhoeck & Ruprecht, Göttingen, 1957), but also *Der Aufbau der geschichtlichen Welt in den Geisteswissenschaften* [1910] and the posthumous *Plan der Fortsetzung zum Aufbau der geschichtlichen Welt in den Geisteswissenschaften*, both included in vol. 7 of the *Gesammelte Schriften* cited in ch. 4 n. 1 above. A more accessible edition of these texts may be found in the volume entitled *Der Aufbau der geschichtlichen Welt in den Geisteswissenschaften*, ed. M. Riedel (Suhrkamp, Frankfurt a.M., 1981).

15 Cf. Gadamer, *Truth and Method*, p. 78.

16 The lecture on 'Hölderlin and the Essence of Poetry' [1936] appears in M. Heidegger, *Existence and Being* (Gateway, Chicago, 1967). The essay 'Wozu Dichter?', originally published in *Holzwege* (Vittorio Klostermann, Frankfurt a.M., 1977), has been translated as 'What are Poets For?' and appears in M. Heidegger, *Poetry, Language, Thought* (Harper & Row, New York, 1971)

pp. 89–142. Cf. also *On the Way to Language* (Harper & Row, New York, 1971).

17 In brief and with considerable simplification. On Heidegger's comments regarding the poets, see the fine study by F. De Alessi, *Heidegger lettore dei poeti* (Rosenberg & Sellier, Turin, 1991).

18 Heidegger, *Existence and Being*, p. 271.

19 Ibid., p. 289: 'Hölderlin writes poetry about the essence of poetry – but not in the sense of a timelessly valid concept. This essence of poetry belongs to a determined time.'

20 For all these quotations, cf. ibid., pp. 288–9.

21 This is Adorno's theory of avant-garde art, for which figures such as Samuel Beckett are representative. On this, see the numerous allusions to Beckett found in *Aesthetic Theory* [1970], trans. C. Lenhardt (Routledge & Kegan Paul, London, 1984).

22 Cf. e.g. the whole of the first section of Gadamer's *The Actuality of the Beautiful* (which gathers together essays from various years between 1967 and 1986), trans. N. Walker, ed. R. Bernasconi (Cambridge Unversity Press, 1986).

23 Cf. e.g. the essay by W. Welsch, 'Das Ästhetische. Eine Schlüsselkategorie unserer Zeit?', in the volume edited by Welsch and containing work by various authors, *Die Aktualität des Ästhetischen* (W. Fink, Munich, 1993). And in addition, R. Bubner, *Aesthetische Erfahrung* [1989] (Suhrkamp, Frankfurt a.M., 1989).

24 This might even lead to a re-evaluation of the museum, with a different orientation to that of 'aesthetic differentiation': see my essay on 'Il museo e l'esperienza dell'arte nella post-modernità' in *Rivista de Estetica*, NS 37 (1991).

Appendix 1   The Truth of Hermeneutics

1 [The primary sense of the Italian *evidenza* is 'clearness', 'obviousness', as opposed to 'the available facts'. In this respect, 'evidentiality' might have been a more accurate translation, but its unwieldiness counselled against. Since the English 'evidence' can be used in the sense intended here, I have therefore chosen to use it in spite of the slight differences in usage that the reader is advised to bear in mind. – Trans.]

2 On the crucial sense of this term in Heidegger, and on the movement of his thinking in the direction of a way out of metaphysics, see the concluding chapter of my *The End of Modernity*, and my contributions to the editions of *Filosofia '86* and *Filosofia '87* (Laterza, Rome-Bari, 1988).

3 In addition to the pages from Gadamer's *Truth and Method* that are dedicated to Heidegger, another important document relating to this point is the interview with Gadamer conducted by Adriano Fabris and published in *Teoria*, fasc. 1 (1982), where Gadamer insists on his closeness to the 'second Heidegger', but also to the idea that the second Heidegger must be drawn back to the first, because it is ultimately a matter of translating into the language of *Being and Time* what was presented in the later works in the form of 'visions'.

4 Cf. Rorty, *Philosophy and the Mirror of Nature*, pp. 315ff.

5 See above, ch. 2, n. 11.
6 Heidegger, 'The Origin of the Work of Art' [1936], in *Poetry, Language, Thought*, pp. 17–87.
7 Cf. Heidegger, *What is Called Thinking?*, p. 33; and Gadamer, *Reason in the Age of Science*, p. 12.
8 Kuhn, *The Structure of Scientific Revolutions*.
9 Cf. again ch. 7 of Rorty, *Philosophy and the Mirror of Nature*.
10 Cf. e.g. Gadamer, *Truth and Method*, pp. 245ff, esp. p. 250.
11 This, for example, is Foucault's position, at least according to Paul Veyne's radical interpretation, which I consider to be exemplary: cf. above all the essay 'È possibile una morale per Foucault?' in *Effetto Foucault*, ed. P. A. Rovatti (Feltrinelli, Milan, 1986), pp. 30–8.
12 See A. McIntyre, *After Virtue* [1981] (Duckworth, London, 1985).
13 For a fuller illustration of this point, see my contribution to the Royaumont colloquium of 1987, 'L'impossible oubli', now included in the volume *Usages de l'oubli*, together with writings by Y. H. Yerushalmi, N. Loraux, H. Mommsen, J. C. Milner (Seuil, Paris, 1988).
14 Cf. the writings referred to in n. 1 above.
15 On the notion of *Erörterung*, a fuller discussion may be found in my *Essere, storia e linguaggio in Heidegger* [1963] (Marietti, Genoa, 1989), esp. ch. 5, pt. 2.
16 [The terms *sfondante* and *sfondamento* have been translated, somewhat clumsily, as 'unfounding' and 'unfoundation' respectively. In Italian, the prefix 's' reverses the sense of the word to which it is attached: e.g. *scontento* (unhappy), *spiaciuto* (displeased) and – significantly – *sfondare* (to break through or knock the bottom – *fondo* – out of something). In the present case, the 'root' words are *fondante* and *fondamento*, that is, 'founding' and 'foundation' respectively. Whilst 'disintegrating' and 'disintegration' were more elegant alternatives, too much of the philosophical sense would probably have been lost. The same point could also be made regarding the Italian *sfondo*, translated here in its customary sense as 'background', which could be thought to signify the contrary of 'fondo', meaning 'bottom' or 'ground'. For an example of where Vattimo exploits this wordplay explicitly cf. *The Transparent Society*, trans. D. Webb (Polity Press, Cambridge, 1992), p. 52. – Trans.]
17 Cf. e.g. the panorama given by I. Hacking, *Representing and Intervening: Introductory Topics in the Philosophy of Science* [1983] (Cambridge University Press, 1983).
18 On the two senses of tradition in Heidegger, see M. Bobnola, *Verità e interpretazzione nello Heidegger di 'Essere e tempo'* (Edizioni di filosofia, Turin, 1983); cf. esp. ch. 5.
19 Derrida, speaking of the 'arbitrary' strategies of the thought of difference, clearly evokes the Mallarméan *coup de dés*, and this is not a purely accidental reference. Cf. 'Différance' in *Margins of Philosophy* [1972], trans. A. Bass (Harvester, Brighton, 1982).
20 In using Lacan's terminology here, I make no claim whatsoever to be faithful to his text; not least since alongside the imaginary and the symbolic, he also posits the 'real', which in my schema seems only to have a place on the side of the imaginary.
21 Cf. K. Mannheim, *Ideology and Utopia*, where a historicist relativism is

tempered by the belief that ideological points of view may be integrated into a 'comprehensive totality' (p. 134) that provides the basis for a scientific politics.
22 On this point, a fuller discussion may be found in my 'Ethics of Communication or Interpretation?' in *The Transparent Society*, pp. 105–20.
23 This is, of course, the thesis of the lecture 'On the Essence of Truth' (which dates from 1930, but was only published in 1943), in M. Heidegger, *Basic Writings*, trans. J. Sallis et al., (Routledge, London, 1993), pp. 115–38.

Appendix 2 The Reconstruction of Rationality

1 Rorty, *Philosophy and the Mirror of Nature*, ch. 7.
2 Cf. Kuhn, *The Structure of Scientific Revolutions*.
3 J. Derrida, *Of Grammatology*, trans. G. Chakravorty Spivak [1967] (Johns Hopkins University Press, Baltimore, 1984).
4 Cf. Gadamer, *Truth and Method*, pp. 267ff.
5 Cf. F. Nietzsche, *The Will to Power*, p. 267.

Index